JACKSONIAN DEMOCRACY

JACKSONIAN DEMOCRACY

Myth or Reality?

Edited by JAMES L. BUGG, Jr.

University of Missouri

THE DRYDEN PRESS

HINSDALE, ILLINOIS

Cover photo of the Jackson statue in Lafayette Park,
Washington, D.C., courtesy National Park Service,
U.S. Department of the Interior.

CONTENTS

CONTENTS

INTRODUCTION

Andrew Jackson shares with Abraham Lincoln the role of the nation's leading folk hero. A man who gloried in the fierce controversy that constantly surrounded him, he engendered during his Presidency a passionate and often irrational loyalty in his followers, who cast him in heroic mould. His enemies, who reacted with a bitter hatred that also often transcended the bounds of logic and reason, pictured him as a crude, unlettered demagogue who manipulated the people that he might mislead and even despoil them. After his death, he continued, as man and myth, to arouse intense feelings among disciples and critics. As the legends, which were forming even before his death, thickened around his name, Jackson and the democratic movement he led became the common property of a host of scholars and pseudo scholars who sought to dissect and to analyze and to explain him. They too, and often against their original intent, entered the ranks of his disciples or those of his foes.

James Parton, the first scholarly biographer of Jackson, collected a mass of conflicting evidence from contemporaries who were still alive in order to publish his three-volume study in 1860. Into its preface he wrote a despairing admission that later scholars have wearily echoed. From the evidence, declared Parton, Jackson could be called both "a patriot and a traitor. He was one of the greatest of generals, and wholly ignorant of the art of war. A writer brilliant, elegant, eloquent, without being able to compose a correct sentence, or spell words of four syllables. The first of statesmen, he never devised, he never framed a measure. He was the most candid of men, and was capable of the profoundest dissimulation. A most law-defying, law-obeying citizen. A stickler for discipline, he never hesitated to disobey his superior. A democratic autocrat. An urbane savage. An atrocious saint." Here, in these few words, lies the essential problem that confronts those who would understand Jackson and the movement which bears his name.

The passing years brought a host of books and articles seeking to enlighten and to clarify, but Jackson remained the controversial figure which Parton had depicted in his preface. Some saw him as the disciple of Jefferson who led the forces of democracy to a triumphant victory over privilege and autocracy;

others believed him a master demagogue intent upon exploiting the credulity of the masses to enhance his power. Those who made him a strong nationalist found others who cast him as the champion of the old Republican virtues of frugality, fiscal solvency, and limited government. To some he appeared a selfless and courageous leader, to others a man duped by clever subordinates bent on exploitation and power.

As with the leader, so with the movement he led. Most scholars have agreed that Jacksonian Democracy was a sprawling, diverse, and many-sided movement. But agreement has ended when discussions of its nature, purposes, and objectives are raised. For some found its origins in the frontier wilderness, while others discovered those origins in the urban centers of the East. Some looked upon its aims as political, while others depicted a more broadly based movement embracing economic, social, and even intellectual objectives. Some found in its major struggles the intent to free Western and Southern farmers from Eastern domination; some viewed them as a revolt of urban—and rural—workers against the domination of a business elite; while others discovered in them a group of entrepreneurs on the make battling a similar group who had already arrived. Its adherents, said some, aimed at creating a utopian future based on political and economic equalitarianism, while others were as certain that the Jacksonians sought the restoration of a golden past, real or imagined.

The persevering reader who endures to the final page will find the selections in this book falling into five general divisions that illustrate the major schools of Jacksonian historiography. James Parton, ablest representative of the early patrician school, spoke for the first generation of Jackson scholars, who wrote during the last half of the nineteenth century. Sharing characteristics common to their Eastern or European backgrounds, they discovered in the Jacksonians men who had defied their traditions of education, social prestige, and the inherent right of qualified families to furnish political leadership. Jackson and his followers, they believed, had disregarded both the claims and the ethics of gentlemen in politics, and his administration therefore furnished a needed object lesson in the degradation of American democracy. They could praise Old Hickory for his nationalism, however, and his *laissez faire* economic policies so congenial to these disciples of Herbert Spencer; some even defended his banking and monetary policies. But they condemned him more for his removal policies, which to their way of thinking became the most important and far-reaching measure of his administration.

In the first three decades of the twentieth century a new group of Jackson scholars contested the evaluations of the patrician school. Deeply influenced by the broad current of reform that characterized the Progressive movement, they viewed Jackson and his democracy in a far more sympathetic spirit. From the pen of Frederick Jackson Turner came a new Jackson who championed the cause of the "upland democracy," conquered the "traditions of conservative rule," and was enthroned as "the idol and the mouthpiece of the popular will."

Turner was a pioneer in the democratic agrarian school of Jackson scholars, whose revisionist analyses provided a new and stimulating interpretation that soon dominated the field of Jacksonian historiography. Easily its most distinguished representative was John Spencer Bassett, the editor of Old Hicksory's correspondence and the author of a scholarly biography. A comparison of his analysis of Jackson with that of Parton provides an insight into the differences that characterized the two schools. The sympathetic yet critical analysis of Bassett was then largely submerged in the frank partisanship of later writers, as the selections of Vernon L. Parrington and Claude Bowers will bear witness. The frontier champion of democracy who stalks through the pages of Parrington almost, but not quite, obscures the suggestion of a significant class struggle that another generation of writers would find central to the understanding of the movement. With Bowers the democratic agrarian thesis reached its most partisan form. Casting aside all shades of gray, Bowers presented a magnificent hero worthy of a Homeric epic, a forest-born Sir Gallahad leading the children of light to triumph over the children of darkness. Jackson became the selfless and noble champion of the common man, fearlessly battling and righteously conquering the forces of privilege, corruption, and oppression.

The revisionists won a great triumph. Their view became the generally accepted interpretation, recorded in a hundred textbooks, repeated from ten thousand political platforms. Yet the victory remained incomplete, for the patrician school refused to die, and a new generation of scholars raised awkward questions. Thomas P. Abernethy wrote of a Jackson whose political career in Tennessee bore little resemblance to the portrait painted by Bowers. A frontier aristocrat and land speculator who opposed the democratic movement in his own state, Jackson emerged on the national level as an opportunist who was neither a consistent politician nor a real leader of democracy. Charles M. Wiltse challenged the Bowers analysis of Jackson's role in the nullification crisis. In place of the invincible unionist, Jackson was portrayed as a petty schemer motivated by his bitter hatred of John C. Calhoun. This new critical school of interpreters stripped Jackson of the heroic pose and reduced him to the level of a scheming vindictive politician.

The publication of the *Age of Jackson* in 1945 was an important milestone in Jacksonian historiography. Arthur Schlesinger, Jr. made the conflict of classes, dimly pictured by Parrington, the principal motivating force of the movement, which he defined as "a second American phase of that enduring struggle between the business community and the rest of society." Thus the East rather than the West furnished the principal stage, the working men rather than the farmers the leading actors. A new and challenging interpretation, the labor school soon bred its own critics, one of the most articulate of whom is Edward Pessen. Not only does he question Schlesinger's belief in a close alliance between organized labor and the Jacksonians, but he further suggests that the political organizations of the workingmen were usually independent of, and often hostile to, the Democratic party.

A fourth school, the entrepreneurial, challenges both the democratic agrarians and the labor proponents. Bray Hammond, one of its leading representatives, discounts the idea of a struggle between agrarians and capitalists, humanity and property, poor and rich, "the people" and "the money power." The real explanation of Jacksonian democracy, he believes, lies in the struggle between two groups of entrepreneurs, a struggle in which state banks played a far larger role than agrarians or labor spokesmen. The Jacksonians, hostile to any exclusion of incipient entrepreneurs from economic opportunities, sought to stimulate business, redistribute vested right, and establish *laissez faire.*

A fifth school enlists the aid of symbolism and psychology to explain the paradox of Jacksonian democracy and its principal hero. Old Hickory, declares John Ward, was a "symbolic figure" created by his contemporaries to embody the characteristic virtues they ascribed to themselves as a people, virtues embodied in the three concepts of God, Nature, and Will. Thus we must distinguish Jackson the historical figure and Jackson the symbol of republican virtue. Marvin Meyers finds the answer in the desire of the Jacksonians "to preserve the virtues of a simple agrarian republic without sacrificing the rewards and conveniences of modern capitalism." They hoped to "reconcile again the simple yeoman values with the free pursuit of economic interest, just as the two were splitting hopelessly apart."

After the reader has considered the analyses of these various scholars, he may conclude with Joseph Blau that "no single statement can cover the variety of positive programs" enunciated by the Jacksonians, for "they were agreed on where they did not want the United States to go, but differed sharply on everything else." Perhaps the reader will join Louis Hartz in proclaiming the typical Jacksonian "both a class conscious democrat and an incipient entrepreneur," at one and the same time a "man of the land, the factory, and the forge." But to whatever conclusions his reading may lead him, the student of Jacksonian democracy will be aware that there have been various and often conflicting analyses by which historians have sought to give meaning to a movement that is central to the American experience. And in seeking to evaluate the many and intricate processes at work in the period, he will discover the real complexities historians face—and learn the danger of oversimplification. Conflicts of interpretation are in fact both inevitable and desirable, for they stimulate renewed efforts to explore the American past. Yet, as Professor Charles Sellers reminds us, "the succession of frames of reference and the multiplication of hypotheses can distort as well as amplify the past."

Two fundamental questions emerge from the material presented here. How does one define and analyze the movement we call Jacksonian democracy?

What role did Andrew Jackson play in this movement? Both the movement and the man who gave it his name are significant to Americans living in another century and in a vastly changed, more complicated nation. The movement occupies a central role in the still developing American political tradition; the man dealt with such familiar problems as presidential power, party politics, and leadership in a democracy. And by no means least, he shares with Thomas Jefferson the role of patron saint of our oldest and largest political party. Historical memories not only tell us where we have been; they can assist us in discovering where we now are, and even where we may be going in the future.

THE ANALYSTS CLASH:
Andrew Jackson

Clever Opportunist

"Democracy was good talk with which to win the favor of the people and thereby accomplish ulterior objectives. Jackson never really championed the cause of the people; he only invited them to champion his."

Thomas P. Abernethy, *From Frontier to Plantation in Tennessee* (Memphis, 1955).

"In four short years Jackson had led his party from bitter opposition to the 'consolidating' tendencies of John Quincy Adams to a form of authoritarianism that outdid even the Alien and Sedition Acts of Adams' father. The individualistic democracy of the frontier lost ground to the cult of power so dear to wealth and property."

Charles M. Wiltse, *John C. Calhoun Nullifier, 1829-1839* (New York, 1949).

or Courageous Democrat

"At last these Western forces of aggressive nationalism and democracy took possession of the government in the person of the man who best embodied them, Andrew Jackson."

Frederick J. Turner, *The Frontier in American History* (New York, 1920; 1962).

"Yet, in a third field came his greatest service—his Homeric battles for the preservation of our democratic institutions and the subordination of money to men in the determination of national policies."

Claude G. Bowers, *Making Democracy a Reality: Jefferson, Jackson, and Polk* (Memphis, 1954).

Jacksonian Democracy

Myth

"The subsequent history of the United States offers no evidence that the influence of wealth was lessened by Jackson's reforms. The sole result of his effort was the elimination of the one bank that had public responsibility for the general welfare and sufficient capital and strength to protect and sustain the national economy. . . . Only the speculators and those so rich that they could not be hurt profited as the nation

6

moved through unrestrained cycles of 'boom and bust' to the financial injury of those who engaged in productive enterprises: farmers, merchants, manufacturers, shippers, bankers, and investors."

    Thomas P. Govan, *Nicholas Biddle: Nationalist and Public Banker 1786-1844* (Chicago, 1959).

"In this direction one can begin to meet the Jacksonian paradox: the fact that the movement which helped to clear the path for laissez-faire capitalism and its culture in America, and the public which in its daily life eagerly entered on that path, held nevertheless in their political conscience an ideal of a chaste republican order, resisting the seductions of risk and novelty, greed and extravagance, rapid motion and complex dealings."

    Marvin Meyers, *The Jacksonian Persuasion: Politics and Belief* (New York, 1960).

"In a society evolving along the American pattern of the Jeffersonian and Jacksonian eras, where the aristocracies, peasantries, and proletariats of Europe are missing, where virtually everyone, including the nascent industrial worker, has the mentality of an independent entrepreneur, two national impulses are bound to make themselves felt; the impulse toward democracy and the impulse toward capitalism. The mass of the people, in other words, are bound to be capitalistic, and capitalism, with its spirit disseminated widely, is bound to be democratic."

    Louis Hartz, *The Liberal Tradition in America: An Interpretation of American Political Thought since the Revolution* (New York, 1955).

or Reality

"Stripped of its incongruous elements, which presently deserted, Jacksonian Democracy was an anti-monopoly party, the enemy of special privilege. . . . Everywhere the less prosperous had been want to attribute their ill fortune to the ruling oligarchy that had run the government in its own interest. For this ailment of the body politic the common man had a sovereign remedy, and he now purposed to administer the medicine to the patient in person."

    Wilfred E. Binkley, *American Political Parties: Their Natural History* (New York, 1943).

"Jacksonian Democracy was rather a second American phase of that enduring struggle between the business community and the rest of society which is the guarantee of freedom in a liberal capitalist state."

    Arthur M. Schlesinger, Jr., *The Age of Jackson* (Boston, 1946).

"With Old Hickory's election a fluid economic and social system broke the bonds of a fixed and stratified political order. Originally a fight against political privilege, the Jacksonian movement had broadened into a fight against economic privilege, rallying to its support a host of 'rural capitalists and village entrepreneurs.'"

    Richard Hofstadter, *The American Political Tradition and the Men Who Made It* (New York, 1949).

I was a man of the people — + he + was a reflection of his times

JAMES PARTON (1822-1891), the nation's first professional biographer, achieved a reputation during the post-Civil War years as one of the more prolific and best-paid authors in the United States. His three-volume life of Jackson illustrates the philosophy of a liberal whose admiration for the man of action is tempered by his disgust with the crudeness and opportunism that characterized popular government. Jefferson and Herbert Spencer were Parton's heroes, rather than Jackson, whom he believed to be a well-intentioned but uneducated leader who erroneously emphasized popular rather than good government, equalitarianism rather than libertarianism. Parton's biography, in spite of its shortcomings, remains an important source for the study of Jackson.*

► ||| **An Evaluation of Andrew Jackson**

Respecting the character of Andrew Jackson and his influence, there will still be differences of opinion. One fact, however, has been established: during the last thirty years of his life, he was the idol of the American people. His faults, whatever they were, were such as a majority of the American citizens of the last generation could easily forgive. His virtues, whatever they were, were such as a majority of American citizens of the last generation could warmly admire. It is this fact which renders him historically interesting. Columbus had sailed; Raleigh and the Puritans had planted; Franklin had lived; Washington fought; Jefferson written; fifty years of democratic government had passed; free schools, a free press, a voluntary church had done

what they could to instruct the people; the population of the country had been quadrupled and its resources increased ten fold; and the result of all was, that the people of the United States had arrived at the capacity of honoring Andrew Jackson before all other living men.

People may hold what opinions they will respecting the merits or importance of this man; but no one can deny that his invincible popularity is worthy of consideration; for what we lovingly admire, that, in some degree, we are. It is chiefly as the representative man of the Fourth-of-July, or combative-rebellious period of American history, that he is interesting to the student of human nature.

Those who have read "Wanderings in

* From James Parton, *Life of Andrew Jackson*, III. Boston: Houghton Mifflin Company, 1888. The first edition was published in 1860.

Corsica" by Gregorovius, will agree with me, that he who would know Napoleon must begin by studying Corsica, which has produced many Napoleons. And no man will ever be able quite to comprehend Andrew Jackson who has not personally known a Scotch-Irishman. More than he was any thing else, he was a North-of-Irelander. A tenacious, pugnacious race; honest, yet capable of dissimulation; often angry, but most prudent when most furious; endowed by nature with the gift of extracting from every affair and every relation all the strife it can be made to yield; at home and among dependents, all tenderness and generosity: to opponents, violent, ungenerous, prone to believe the very worst of them; a race that means to tell the truth, but, when excited by anger or warped by prejudice, incapable of either telling, or remembering, or knowing the truth; not taking kindly to culture, but able to achieve wonderful things without it; a strange blending of the best and the worst qualities of two races. Jackson had these traits in an exaggerated degree; as Irish as though he were not Scotch; as Scotch as though he were not Irish.

The circumstances of his childhood nourished his peculiarities. He was a poor boy in a new country, without a father to teach him moderation, obedience, and self-control. The border warfare of the Revolution whirled him hither and thither; made him fierce and exacting; taught him self-reliance; accustomed him to regard an opponent as a foe. They who are not for us are against us, and they who are against us are to be put to death, was the Carolina doctrine during the later years of the war. The early loss of his elder brother, his own hard lot in the Camden prison, the terrible and needless sufferings of his younger brother, the sad but heroic

death of his mother, were events not calculated to give the softer traits the mastery within him. All the influences of his early years tended to develop a very positive cast of character, to make him self-helpful, decisive, indifferent to danger, impatient of contradition, and disposed to follow up a quarrel to the death. Not to be of *his* party was to be a traitor, and death was too good for traitors.

⌐His first step in life shows something of the quality of the man.⌐ His father, his forefathers, his relatives in Carolina, had all walked the lowlier paths of life, and aspired to no other. This poor, gaunt, and sickly orphan places himself at once upon the direct road to the higher spheres. He gets a little money by teaching school, mounts his horse, and rides away to the North to find a chance to study law. He accomplishes his purpose with playful ease. After two years of the most boisterous jollity, the tradition of which is fresh in Salisbury to this day, he has won his license to practice, and goes off, penniless, to regions unknown. He lingers a year in the old settlements; long enough to discover that there is no room there for a lad of his mettle.

Westward, ho! Half a dozen young lawyers go with him to the valley of the Cumberland, but *he* has contrived to get an appointment as prosecuting solicitor, an office supposed to be worse than valueless; but he made it invaluable. He becomes at once a man of mark in the new country. The little settlement existed in a state of siege, liable to attack at ~~every moment~~ by day and night. Every clump of trees, every thicket of cane, every field of corn, might conceal a foe. Every mile of every journey had its own peculiar peril. The solicitor, half the year on horseback, compelled to make long and solitary journeys, lived in an atmosphere of danger, and became habituated to self-reliance. Always escaping, he learned to confide implicitly in his star; believing that no harm could befall if Andrew Jackson was near. To the last hour of his life this was his habitual feeling.

This kind of life may make men tender and amiable at home, because they are always *protecting* its beloved inmates; but abroad, in their intercourse with men, they become direct, fierce, clannish. Their feelings are primitive and intense. They use "the English language." If a man varies from the truth, they call him a liar without more ado, and the man who is called a liar can only clear his character by fighting. A word and a blow becomes the law of the wilderness. And in a country where fighting is one of the necessities of every man's lot, the man readiest to fight and ablest in fight, is necessarily the first man.

How prompt Mr. Solicitor Jackson was with vituperative word and rectifying pistol, we all know. While yet a boy he notifies Commissary Galbraith to prepare for another world before attempting to execute his threat of chastisement. Offended in the court-room at Jonesborough by Mr. Avery's harmless satire, he tears a blank leaf from a law book and dashes off a challenge, which he himself delivers; and, before the sun sets, the duel has been fought, and the antagonists are friends again. The affair with Dickinson was of a very different nature. So far as the *written* testimony enables us to judge, Jackson was wholly, grossly, abominably in the wrong. But the tradition in the circle of Jackson's nearest friends is clear and strong, that Dickinson had reviled Mrs. Jackson in his cups. . . .

[Jackson had passed his forty-fifth year without having achieved any thing very remarkable.] Public life he had tried,

but had not shone in it, and nothing became him in his public life so much as his leaving it. He had tried merchandising, but not successfully. He tried speculation in land, and nearly lost all his estate by his ignorance of law, but saved it, at the last moment, by one of his characteristic spurts of energy. [Nothing really prospered with him but his farm and his horses, both of which he loved, and, therefore, understood.] Upon the whole, however, he had shown himself a leader of the people, helping them, at each turn of his career, to what they wanted most: first, law; then, merchandise; next, horses; lastly, defense.

The massacre at Fort Mims [Alabama]* gave him, at length, a piece of work which he was better fitted to do than any other man in the world. Only such energy, such swiftness, such resolution, such tenacity of purpose, such disregard of forms and precedents, such audacity, and such prudence as his, could have defended the Southwest in 1814 and 1815. When a man successfully defends his invaded country, we must not too closely scrutinize the acts which dim the luster of his great achievement. The captain who *saves* his imperiled ship we honor, though, in the critical hour, he may have sworn like a trooper, and knocked down a man or two with the speaking trumpet. The slaying of the six militiamen, and the maintaining of martial law in New Orleans two months too long, we may condemn, and, I think, should condemn; yet most of the citizens of the United States will concur in the wish, that when next a European army lands upon American soil, there may be a Jackson to meet them at the landing-place. After making all proper deduc-

---

* The massacre took place on August 30, 1813. Over 400 men, women, and children were killed by the Creek Indians—Ed.

tions, justice still requires that we should accord to General Jackson's defense of the southern country the very highest praise. It was a piece of difficult work most gloriously done. Not even the party celebrations of the eighth of January ought to hide from us or obscure the genuine merit of those who, in the darkest hour this republic has ever known, enabled it to believe again in its invincibility, by closing a war of disaster in a blaze of triumph.

He came home from the wars the pride, the darling of the nation. No man in this country has ever been subjected to such a torrent of applause, and few men have been less prepared to withstand it by education, reflection, and experience. He accepted the verdict which the nation pronounced upon his conduct. Well pleased with himself, and with his countrymen, he wrote those lofty letters to Mr. Monroe [especially one dated November 12, 1816], the burthen of which is that a President of the United States should rise superior to party spirit, appoint no man to office for party reasons, but be the President of the whole people, judging every applicant for presidential favor by his conduct alone. His feud with [General John] Adair, and his quarrel with General [Winfield] Scott, soon showed that, with all his popularity and his fine words, he was the same Andrew Jackson as of old, unable to bear opposition, and prone to believe the worst of those who did not yield to him implicitly. He went to Florida in 1818, burthened and stimulated with a stupendous military reputation. The country expected great things of the victor of New Orleans, and the victor of New Orleans was not a man to disappoint his country. He swept down into the province like a tornado, and drove the poor remnant of the Seminoles into the Everglades. He assumed, he exercised all the prerogatives of an absolute' sovereign. He raised troops in his own way; invaded a foreign territory; made war upon his brother sovereign, the King of Spain; put his subjects to death without trial; shot [Robert C.] Ambrister, and permitted the murder of [Alexander] Arbuthnot [both British subjects]. He came home, not in chains, to stand his trial for such extraordinary proceedings, but in triumph, to receive the approval of the President, defense and eulogy from John Quincy Adams, exoneration from Congress, and the applause of the people. What an effect such an experience as this was likely to have upon such a mind as his, we need not say.

He reappeared in Florida as its Governor. We may palliate and forgive his conduct there in 1821. It must, nevertheless, be pronounced violent, arrogant, and disgraceful to the civilization of his country. Every unbiased gentleman who witnessed his performances at Pensacola in 1821, beheld them with mingled wonder and disgust. All his worst qualities were inflamed by disease and disappointment. He laid about him like a madman.

He was started for the presidency. He was passive; he was clay in the hands of two or three friendly potters. Tennessee took up his name with enthusiasm; Pennsylvania brought it prominently before the nation; he wrote his tariff letter [to Dr. L. H. Colman, dated April 26, 1824]; he voted for internal improvements; the Monroe correspondence was published; he won a plurality of electoral votes, but was not elected. His disappointment was keen, and his wrath burned anew and with increased fury against the man who had given the office to Mr. Adams. If he did not invent the bargain-and-corruption lie, he did worse, he believed it. To be willing to believe so scandalous a tale respecting such men, except upon what may strictly be called *evidence,* is not creditable to the heart or the understanding of any man. To persist in believing it for fifteen years, after it had been completely disproved, to avow a belief in it, for political purposes, just as he was sinking into the grave, revealed a phase of character which we have a right to call detestable. We owe it to the interests of human nature to execrate such conduct.

If General Jackson was passive during the campaign of 1824, he was passive no longer. The exposure of the circumstances attending his marriage, accompanied by unjust comments and gross exaggerations, the reflections upon his mother, the revival of every incident of his life that could be unfavorably construed, kept him in a blaze of wrath. Determined to triumph, he took an active part, at home and abroad, in the canvass. He was elected; but, in the moment of his triumph, his wife, than whom no wife was ever more tenderly beloved, was lost to him for ever. The calamity that robbed life of all its charm deepened, and, as it were, sanctified his political resentments! His enemies had slain her, he thought. Adams had permitted, if he had not prompted, the circulation of the calumnies that destroyed her. Clay, he firmly believed, had originated the crusade against her; for this strange being could believe any evil thing of one whom he cordially hated. Broken in spirit, broken in health, the old man, cherishing what he deemed a holy wrath, but meaning to serve his country well, went to Washington, to find it crowded with hungry claimants for reward.

Oh, what an opportunity was his! Oh,

if he could but have buried the hateful past in oblivion, and risen to the height of his letters to Mr. Monroe! Or, if he could only have devised some other mode of avenging his private wrongs! How different were the condition of public affairs in this year 1860, how different the prospect before us, if, instead of that vague and ominous paragraph about "reform," in his inaugural address, he had used language like this:

"KNOW, all whom it may concern, that in this republic no man should seek, few men should decline, a public trust. To apply for office, fellow-citizens, is of itself an evidence of unfitness for office. I will appoint no man to an office who seeks one, or for whom one is sought. When I want a man, I shall know how to find him. If any one has indulged the expectation that I will deprive honest and capable men of their places because they thought proper to oppose my election to the presidency, and, in the heat of an exciting canvass, went beyond the limits of a fair and proper opposition, I notify them now and here, that Andrew Jackson, imperfect and faulty as he is, is not capable of conduct so despicable. Depart hence, ye office-seeking crew, whose very presence here shows that your motives for supporting me were base!"

Such a paragraph as this would have astonished the office-seekers; but the people would have sustained him, would now sustain any president who should utterly defy the office-seeking horde.

General Jackson's appointment-and-removal policy I consider an evil so great and so difficult to remedy, that if all his other public acts had been perfectly wise and right, this single feature of his administration would suffice to render it deplorable rather than admirable. The captain of a ship who should be, ever and anon, going below and secretly boring a hole in the hull, where it could be reached only with the greatest difficulty, and stopped with greater, we should esteem a bad captain, even though he sailed his ship well, and, upon occasion, fought her valiantly. Something like this General Jackson did to the ship of state; and ever since his day the crew have had hard pumping; and we still continue to pump, instead of going into dock and overhauling her bottom, and stopping the leaks, and putting on new copper so thick that no future captain will be able to get his augur through it. Let no one hope for decency or honesty in the government while the servants of the public hold their places at the mercy of the successful wire-puller. [Rotation ? necessitates corruption, organizes corruption, appears almost to justify corruption. The ship needs repairing infinitely more than the officers need changing.]

When a man in high office acts upon principles diametrically contrary to those which he professed in private life, we are apt to infer that his professions were hypocritical. Such an inference, in the case before us, would be worse than uncharitable; it would be erroneous. Unquestionably General Jackson wrote his fine letters to Mr. Monroe with perfect sincerity, little thinking that he would ever be called upon to act upon the high principles he laid down for the guidance of another. But what is easier than to write lofty sentiments? Men do not much differ in their knowledge of what is right; it is in our power to act up to our knowledge that we differ from one another. Take the most eloquent of the northern heroes of the platform; take the fiercest of the fire-eaters; make one of them, no matter which, emperor of the United States, clothed with power to carry out the ideas with which twenty years of

advocacy have made him and us familiar. Where were then his readiness, his confidence, his fluency? How overwhelming the thought, that a mistake of his, trifling as it might seem, applauded as it would be, would affect the welfare of millions of human beings for many ages! Ah! how easy to thrill an audience with glowing sentences, but how difficult, in any province of human affairs, to effect even a slight improvement! I do not accuse Jackson of hypocrisy. He had force enough to carry out a purpose of his own, but not that nobler force which enables men to act upon the high principles in public life which they had approved in private. Influenced at once by his resentments, by gratitude, by the opinions of the New York politicians, by the clamors of the hungry crowd of office-seekers, he seems to have fallen without a struggle.

Many, very many, of the measures of General Jackson's administration will always be heartily approved by a majority of the people of the United States. Some of these were the result of his own sagacity and experience; others were due to the Jeffersonian opinions imbibed in their youth by Mr. Van Buren, Mr. [Edward] Livingston, Col. [Thomas Hart] Benton, and others. The removal of the Indians, the policy of selling the public lands to actual settlers only and at the bare cost of selling, were the President's own ideas, I believe. With regard to the war upon the Bank of the United States, every one is glad the bank was destroyed, but no one can admire the manner or the spirit in which the war was waged. At the same time, it is not clear that any other kind of warfare could have been successful against an institution so rooted in the country as that was in 1829.

There is a passage in Mr. [Henry

Thomas] Buckle's colossal work, the "History of Civilization in England," which will occur to some as they read of General Jackson and his administration. Gladly do I borrow a few sentences from a writer whose advent is an era in the history of man. "There is no instance on record," says Mr. Buckle, "of an ignorant man who, having good intentions and supreme power to enforce them, has not done far more evil than good. And where the intentions have been very eager and the power very extensive, the evil has been enormous. But if you can diminish the sincerity of that man, if you can mix some alloy with his motives, you will likewise diminish the evil which he works. If he is selfish as well as ignorant, it will often happen that you may play off his vice against his ignorance, and by exciting his fears restrain his mischief. If, however, he has no fear, if he is entirely unselfish, if his sole object is the good of others, if he pursues that object with enthusiasm, upon a large scale, and with disinterested zeal, then it is that you have no check upon him, you have no means of preventing the calamities which, in an ignorant age, an ignorant man will be sure to inflict."

I must avow explicitly the belief, that, notwithstanding the good done by General Jackson during his presidency, his elevation to power was a mistake on the part of the people of the United States. The good which he effected has not continued; while the evil which he began remains, has grown more formidable, has now attained such dimensions that the prevailing feeling of the country, with regard to the corruptions and inefficiency of the government, is despair. I will also avow the opinion, that, of all men sent to Washington, the man surest to fall a prey to the worse influences of the place is your honest country gentleman, whose intentions are excellent and whose ignorance is almost as complete as his innocence. I find in General Jackson's private writings no evidence that he had ever studied the art of governing nations, or had arrived at any clear conclusions on the subject. Except the "Vicar of Wakefield" it is doubtful if he had ever read any secular book through. That solitary exception is creditable to his taste and feelings as a human being, for no man can be altogether despicable who keenly relishes the "Vicar of Wakefield." But a President of the United States should know all books, all times, all nations, all arts, all artifices, all men. It is essential that he be a man of culture. His culture may not prevent his falling into error, but a cultivated man is capable of being convinced of his errors. He can not *be* a cultivated man without having learned, over and over again, how fallible his judgment is; without having often been *sure* that he was right and then found that he was wrong. It must be admitted, that General Jackson, when his purpose was formed, when his feelings were roused, was not capable of being convinced. His will tyrannized over him, over his friends, over Congress, over the country. No Dionysius of old was more the autocrat that he. Unapproachable by an honest opponent, he could be generally wielded by any man who knew how to manage him, and was lavish enough of flattery.

Andrew Jackson, in fact, was a fighting man, and little more than a fighting man. It was not till a political controversy became personalized, that his force and strength were elicited. He hated the whig party much, but Henry Clay more; nullification much, but Calhoun more; the bank much, but Biddle more. He was a thorough-going human fighting-cock—very kind to the hens of his own farm-yard, giving them many a nice kernel of corn, but bristling up at the faintest crow of chanticleer on the other side of the road.

There are certain historical facts which puzzle and disgust those whose knowledge of life and men has been chiefly derived from books. To such it can with difficulty be made clear that the award is just which assigns to George Washington a higher place than Benjamin Franklin and Thomas Jefferson—higher honor to the executing hand than to the conceiving head. If they were asked to mention the greatest Englishman of this age, it would never occur to them to name the Duke of Wellington, a man of an understanding so limited as to be the natural foe of every thing liberal and progressive. Yet the Duke of Wellington was the only Englishman of his generation to whom every Englishman took off his hat. And these men of books contemplate with mere wonder the fact, that during a period when Webster, Clay, Calhoun, [William] Wirt, and [William C.] Preston were on the public stage, Andrew Jackson should have been so much the idol of the American people, that all those eminent men united could not prevail against him in a single instance.

It is pleasant to justify the ways of man to man. The instinctive preferences of the people must be right. That is to say, the man preferred by the people must have more in him of what the people most want than any other of his generation. The more intimately we know the men who surrounded General Washington, the clearer to us does his intrinsic superiority become, and the more clearly we preceive his utter indispensableness. Washington was the only man of the revolution who did for the revolution what no other man could

have done. And if ever the time comes when the eminent contemporaries of Andrew Jackson shall be as intimately known to the people as Andrew Jackson now is, the invincible preference of the people for him will be far less astonishing than it now appears. . . .

The Washingtons, the Wellingtons, and the Jacksons of a nation are they who provide or preserve for all other gifts, talents, and virtues, their opportunity and sphere. How just, therefore, is the gratitude of nations toward those who, at the critical moment, DO the great act that creates or defends them! . . .

It was curious that England and America should both, and nearly at the same time, have elevated their favorite generals to the highest civil station. Wellington became prime minister in 1827; Jackson, President in 1829. Wellington was tried three years, and found wanting, and driven from power, execrated by the people. His carriage, his house, and his statue were pelted by the mob. Jackson reigned eight years, and retired with his popularity undiminished. The reason was, that Wellington was not in accord with his generation, and was surrounded by men who were, if possible, less so; while Jackson, besides being in sympathy with the people, had the great good fortune to be influenced by men who had learned the rudiments of statesmanship in the school of Jefferson.

Yes, autocrat as he was, Andrew Jackson loved the people, the common people, the sons and daughters of toil, as truly as they loved him, and believed in them as they believed in him.

He was in accord with his generation. He had a clear perception that the toiling millions are not a class in the community, but *are* the community. He knew and felt that government should exist only for the benefit of the governed;

that the strong are strong only that they may aid the weak; that the rich are rightfully rich only that they may so combine and direct the labors of the poor as to make labor more profitable to the laborer. He did not comprehend these truths as they are demonstrated by Jefferson and [Herbert] Spencer, but he had an intuitive and instinctive perception of them. And in his most autocratic moments, he really thought that he was fighting the battle of the people, and doing their will while baffling the purposes of their representatives. If he had been a man of knowledge as well as force, he would have taken the part of the people more effectually, and left to his successors an increased power of doing good, instead of better facilities for doing harm. He appears always to have meant well. But his ignorance of law, history, politics, science, of every thing which he who governs a country ought to know, was extreme. Mr. [Nicholas P.] Trist remembers hearing a member of the General's family say, that General Jackson did not believe the world was round. His ignorance was as a wall round about him—high, impenetrable. He was imprisoned in his ignorance, and sometimes raged round his little, dim enclosure like a tiger in his den.

The calamity of the United States has been this: the educated class have not been able to accept the truths of the democratic creed. They have followed the narrow, conservative, respectable Hamilton—not the large, liberal, progressive Jefferson. But the people have instinctively held fast to the Jeffersonian sentiments. Hence, in this country, until very recently, the men of books have had little influence upon public affairs; and at this moment the spirit that prevails in very many institutions of learning in the country is at war, open, declared war, with the spirit of democracy. And if, at the present time, there is a class of intelligent and instructed men who feel with the people, and are striving for popular objects, the fact is not due, in any degree whatever, to the colleges. For fifty years the spectacle was exhibited in the United States of two parties—one composed chiefly of the educated and wealthy, and the other chiefly of the men who labor with their hands. The old federal party was the rich man's party; the old democratic party was the poor man's party; and of all the various differences between them, this was the most real and essential one. Therefore, the cultivated intellect of the country had little to do with directing its policy and amending its laws. The consequences have been that, as a general rule, the educated American of leisure has been the most aimless and useless of human beings, and the public affairs of the United States have been conducted with a stupidity which has excited the wonder of mankind. To this most lamentable divorce between the people and those who ought to have been worthy to lead them, and who *would* have led them if they had been worthy, we are to attribute the elevation to the presidency of a man whose ignorance, whose good intentions, and whose passions combined to render him, of all conceivable human beings, the most unfit for the office. But those who concur in the opinion that the administration of Andrew Jackson did more harm than good to the country—the harm being permanent, the good evanescent—should never for a moment forget that it was the people of the United States who elected him to the presidency. *a defense J.J.*

LEONARD D. WHITE (1891-1958), until his death
professor of Public Administration at the University of
Chicago, was a recognized authority in this field.
His collective works on administrative history span
the years from 1789 to 1901 and present an excellent
picture of the organization and practical operation
of the United States government. His scholarly
and temperate analysis of the Jacksonian patronage
policy furnishes a needed corrective to the dramatic
and lurid charges that Parton made and demonstrates
the overemphasis he placed on this aspect of the
Jackson administration.*

Andrew Jackson and the Administrative System

Jackson's loyalty to his friends was not always conducive to success in administration, particularly since this loyalty sometimes obscured his judgment in making appointments and refusing to make removals. He appointed Samuel Swartwout** collector of the port of New York although Van Buren warned him against his choice. He put Major John H. Eaton in the Cabinet despite his knowledge of disquieting rumors about the Major's earlier relations with Peggy Timberlake, now his wife, and wrecked his Cabinet as a consequence.

** Swartwout, one of the poorest and probably the most notorious of the Jackson appointees, proved to be both a lax administrator and a thief. After serving eight years as collector at the New York customhouse, he sailed for England; he had stolen in all $1,225,705 69—Ed.

He endured William T. Barry as Postmaster General long after his incompetence had been exposed. Even a President as independent and forthright as Andrew Jackson did not have a free hand in picking executive heads and subordinate officers, and some of his mistakes may be charged to force of circumstances and pressure of party. Some of his mistakes were his own; and his greatest successes—such as Martin Van Buren and Amos Kendall—were often happy chances. He knew neither man personally when he decided to appoint him. In building his civil administration Jackson tended to judge men by their political faith and personal loyalty, not by their executive talent.

The consequences of the Jacksonian

* Reprinted with the permission of the publisher from *The Jacksonians: A Study in Administrative History, 1829-1861* by Leonard D. White, copyright 1954 by The Macmillan Company. Footnotes omitted or renumbered by permission.

era (1829-61) upon administration were manifold, but to an intelligent and informed observer like Amos Kendall the net result of thirty-years development must have seemed a substantial retrogression. The deterioration is often charged against Jackson, as the originator of the spoils system. Such a conclusion would be unjust. Jackson did introduce *rotation* into the federal system for reasons which carried weight in the light of the situation that had grown up in the first forty years of national experience. He did not introduce the spoils system. His personal standards of integrity were fastidious, and he insisted upon a high level of honesty and propriety in the public service. He was betrayed by some officials, and his views of official conduct were undermined by a general decline in business morality. But Jackson would have been as violent an enemy of "honest graft," favoritism, waste, misuse of public funds for party purposes, and outright embezzlement as any of his contemporaries, Whig or Democrat. The idea of rotation was a rational remedy in 1829 for an admitted problem of superannuation, but the cure introduced evils of greater proportion. Jackson may well be criticized for failing to see the consequences of the theory of rotation which were obvious both to intelligent friends and enemies. He can hardly be criticized for the purposes he sought to achieve—to destroy the idea of property in office, to cut down an officeholding class, and to give all citizens an equal opportunity to enjoy the privilege of participating in the task of self-government. . . .

* * * *

Forty years of substantially steady practice prior to 1829 had established a tradition of permanence and stability in the public service of the federal government. Washington and Adams, Jefferson after a couple years of adjustment, Madison, Monroe, and John Quincy Adams all assumed that no man was subject to discharge for difference in political opinion or for a free expression of his political views. Appointments to fill vacancies, caused most often by death of an incumbent, were regularly taken from the ranks of Republicans after 1801, but many Federalists quietly held office without disturbance; and both Republicans and Federalists were gentlemen. Adams had resolutely refused to allow the Tenure of Office Act to be used for political purposes and had steadfastly reappointed both friend and foe as commissions expired. If one could discount the patronage ferment in New York and Pennsylvania, one might have concluded in 1828 that the tradition of permanence and stability was as well established as the two-term tradition of the presidency.

Events subsequent to 1829 exploded such a comfortable assumption. Many circumstances combined to shake, but not wholly to destroy, the old tradition. Much more was involved than the will of one man, or the animosity that existed between the two wings of the Republican party, or even the ardor for office that boiled up during those years. A new sense of democracy was brewing, and a belief that self-government required wide participation by citizens, not only in legislative halls but in executive offices. In the state and local governments this belief was effectuated by the direct election of most officeholders. In the federal government this solution was impossible, short of constitutional amendment. Rotation was an alternative.

Quite apart from theory and disquisition, . . . the old stability in officeholding was threatened by the voice of the people themselves. The demand for appointments grew apace, and local politicians did not hesitate to tell their successful partisans in places of authority what they expected. Rotation was imposed because it was demanded from below, not merely because it was advocated from above. . . .

* * * *

The breeze that Daniel Webster had prophesied began to blow in the spring of 1829. In anticipation of being displaced, anxiety and apprehension mounted among the government clerks and agents. In his diary of May 1, 1829, John Quincy Adams wrote, "Every one is in breathless expectation, trembling at heart, and afraid to speak. Some of the dismissions are deserved: from age, from incapacity, from intemperance, from irregularities of private life; and these are made the pretext for justifying all the removals. The persons appointed are of equally various characters—some good, the greater part very indifferent, some notoriously bad—on the average, much less respectable than those dismissed."

James Parton described the psychological upheaval in vivid terms. "Terror, meanwhile, reigned in Washington. . . . The great body of officials awaited their fate in silent horror, glad when the office hours expired at having escaped another day. . . . No man deemed it safe and prudent to trust his neighbor, and the interior of the department presented a fearful scene of guarded silence, secret intrigue, espionage, and tale-bearing."

"A clerk in the War Office, named Henshaw," Adams wrote in his diary, "who was a strong partisan for Jackson's election, three days since cut his throat from ear to ear, from the mere terror of being dismissed. Linneus Smith, of the Department of State, one of the best

clerks under the Government, has gone raving distracted, and others are said to be threatened with the same calamity."

The shock was undoubtedly great, but the statistics show that the number of removals, although unprecedented, was small in terms of percentage. An early reckoning of gains and losses, which is generally accepted as the most reliable indication of the number of removals during the months when they were in full swing, was published in the Washington *Telegraph* on September 27, 1830. The editor declared that the list had been compiled "with the most sedulous care, and authenticated by a reference, in each individual case, to the Public Departments." It was reprinted in 1832 by the *Globe*, then the administration paper, with a statement that the general accuracy of the list had never been questioned.[1] These figures showed a total of 919 removals out of 10,093 officeholders or somewhat less than 10 per cent.

They represent the situation as of early autumn 1830, after about eighteen months of the new administration. They indicate the magnitude of the "proscription," for subsequent changes were made principally as vacancies occurred by death, resignation, lapse of commission at the end of a four-year term, or on ground of proved delinquency. Eriksson was not able to present figures for the rest of Jackson's administration, but concluded that less than 20 per cent of all officeholders were removed, and that probably the figure was nearer 10 per cent.[2]

[1] Erik McKinley Eriksson, "The Federal Civil Service under President Jackson," *Mississippi Valley Historical Review*, XIII (1926-27), 527-28.

[2] Another view of Jackson's record on removals arises from considering the presidential offices only. Fish discovered that of an approximate total of 612 such officers, 252 were removed during his two terms. [Carl R. Fish,] *Civil Service and the Patronage*, p. 125.

The evidence of the figures published in the *Telegraph* and the careful study by Eriksson show that the "reform" was far from a clean sweep. Many office-holders who saw Jackson inaugurated on March 4, 1829, were of course his partisans. The proportion is now impossible to calculate. Among the clerks in the Post Office Department in Washington, Abraham Bradley reported that 17 were Jackson men, 21 Adams men, and 5 were neutral. Many other clerks and agents who, in accordance with old tradition, had remained neutral during the campaign of 1828 were left in peace. John Quincy Adams, who would rate as a credible witness on this point, wrote in his diary at the end of 1830 that Samuel Swartwout, the new collector at the port of New York, had refused to remove any of the Adams men in the customhouse, and had been attacked on this ground by Van Buren's paper, the *New York Courier and Enquirer*. Such restraint was not long to endure, however, in these green pastures.

The abandonment of old ideas of tenure during good behavior was well illustrated in Postmaster General Barry's letter to Nathaniel Mitchell, postmaster at Portland, Maine, announcing his removal.

As your official conduct had met with my decided approbation, not only in reference to the discharge of your ordinary duties, but also in respect to the performance of a difficult service that had devolved on you as the special agent of the department, and which you had attended to with commendable zeal and fidelity, I have all along cherished the hope that the circumstances of the case would be such as would justify your retention. But it is obvious that the public sentiment in Maine demands a change in the office. . . .

The situation of Martin Van Buren when he entered the White House in 1837 as successor to Andrew Jackson did not suggest the virtue of rotating Jackson's friends out of office, and relatively few removals were made. In 1837 he removed only one presidential postmaster; in 1838 only two. His Postmaster General, Amos Kendall, announced in 1837 that he would not remove postmasters, whatever their political opinions, if they were good, faithful, and quiet. "All the support I ask for the administration from postmasters is a faithful, polite, and obliging performance of their duties, contenting themselves with the exercise of their own rights without attempting to proselyte others." At the end of two years he had removed 364 postmasters; there were then about 12,000 post offices. Van Buren's removals in 1839 and 1840, when he was looking forward to a second term, suggested, however, that a new rule of personal allegiance, as well as party membership, was to be required of officeholders.

The crucial test would be the behavior of the Whigs, who carried the election of 1840 after a campaign in which, if any issue could be discovered, it was reform—reform in the sense of the old Republican tradition. Not much was known of Harrison's views, but in a letter written prior to the election of 1836 he declared that executive power was granted for the public interest and "not to requite personal favors or gratify personal animosities." According to the Washington *Madisonian* (March 22, 1841), Harrison warmly refused to yield to the importunities of "three or four leading Whigs" who were urging the immediate discharge of Democratic officeholders. Around the Cabinet table sat Daniel Webster and Thomas Ewing, who had taken a conspicuous part in the great debate of 1835 against the theory of rotation; and the Vice President, John Tyler, was a stern old Republican from Virginia. Would now the tide sweeping the country to corruption and despotism be turned? Would now the public service become again an institution serving the country irrespective of the party in power? Would the invincible power of the Executive, buttressed by a corps of one hundred thousand dependents, be cropped? These were the questions the Whigs had raised against Jackson, and their day of reckoning was at hand.

Whatever the personal repugnance of the chief actors, the Cabinet decided during March 1841 to make an extensive change of personnel throughout the service. Ewing found justification in the actions of the departing Van Buren Dèmocrats. "It had been the policy of the party just thrust from power," he wrote in his diary, "to retain in office none but their *active* political adherents, those who would go for them thorough in all things; and the performance of official duty, was far less requisite to a tenure of office, than electioneering services. Hence the offices had become for the most part filled with brawling offensive political partisans, of a very low moral standard—their official duties performed by substitutes, or not performed at all." Henry Clay was no help; he asked for removals in order to place his personal friends, and Postmaster General Francis Granger was active in changing the party complexion of the postal establishment. In the six months he held office he removed 39 of the 133 presidential postmasters, and by September 1841 almost 2,500 postmasters had been appointed in the lesser offices to vacancies most of

which were caused by removals. Granger later boasted that he had removed 1,700 postmasters and had he remained two or three weeks longer, would have removed 3,000 more.

John Tyler, succeeding Harrison almost immediately, took high ground in his inaugural address to Congress, declaring that he would make no removals of faithful and honest incumbents except those guilty of active partisanship. But in 1842 he ordered the removal of some thirty measurers and weighers in the Philadelphia customhouse to make room for his men. Fish concluded his study of the Harrison–Tyler administration by declaring that the Whigs adopted all the characteristic practices of the spoils system. "Their leaders were indifferent; either willingly or perforce they permitted a repetition of the deeds which they had so violently condemned."...

The details and the approximate number of removals as Polk succeeded Tyler, himself to give way to Taylor, and as Pierce and Buchanan carried the Democrats into office for two consecutive terms need not detain us. Both Whig and Democratic administrations followed the practice of Jackson. The full application of the theory of rotation came with Buchanan. The Pierce officeholders had worked for Pierce's renomination—but they were Democrats and presumably had supported Buchanan in his successful contest against the Republican candidate, [John C.] Frèmont. Were they now to be spared, as Democrats, or decapitated, as Pierce men? Buchanan stood squarely on the doctrine of rotation and announced that no one would receive reappointment after his commission expired, unless under exceptional circumstances. To his friend, John Y. Mason, he wrote after his election was assured,

"They say, and that, too, with considerable force, that if the officers under a preceding Democratic administration shall be continued by a succeeding administration of the same political character, this must necessarily destroy the party. This, perhaps, ought not to be so, but we cannot change human nature." [William L.] Marcy wrote on March 27, 1857, "Strange things have been enacted here during the last three weeks. Pierce men are hunted down like wild beasts." The theory of rotation had finally been perfected. The triumph of the new system was complete in civilian circles. No one thought to remember the days of the old Republicans nor the care with which they had preserved the character of the public service above faction and party....

The years immediately succeeding the departure of Andrew Jackson from Washington were, therefore, crucial. A long period of political stability might have reproduced the Jeffersonian tradition. This happy circumstance was not to occur. The Whigs carried the 1840 election; the Democrats returned in 1844 only to be thrown out again in the election of 1848. The Whigs lost in 1852 and it was not until then that the Democrats were able to remain in office for two consecutive terms. They were defeated in 1860 by a new national party that had never held the presidency. No sequence of events could have been more conducive to coerce party leaders to apply the doctrine of rotation.

Nevertheless, despite these untoward circumstances and in defiance of the rule of rotation, the old Federalist–Republican practice of a permanent service persisted in some measure. A duel system was in operation from 1829 to 1861, one sector partisan, rotating its personnel; the other, based in part on examinations and in part on custom, neutral and permanent....

*   *   *   *

From 1789 to 1829 a single type of public service had existed that may properly be designated a career system. Without any formal method of selection and with no guarantees other than custom, the system stood unchallenged for forty years. Young men began as clerks, and most of them continued to toil as clerks in the office in which they entered, except for the few who became principal clerks or chief clerks. They had the assets of correct habits, complete knowledge of their small world, and official reliability.

After 1829 this simple, single system bifurcated under the influence of the theory of rotation. It was not, however, destroyed. Old-time clerks remained at their desks; "party" clerks came and went. The toughness of administrative systems was again exemplified as the career system continued despite the handicaps to which it was exposed and the sudden blows it received every four years from 1840 to 1860.

Two personnel systems were thus in operation in the public service. The patronage system held the public attention, but it was primarily the career system that enabled the government to maintain its armed forces, to collect its revenue, to operate its land system, to keep its accounts and audit its expenditures. The patronage system had a fatal defect, because it possessed a double loyalty—one to the executive branch, the other to the political party. It also had a unique asset, because it enabled many citizens to participate in the business of government. The adjustment of the two systems remained even a century later an object of concern.

JOHN SPENCER BASSETT (1867-1928), a leading American historian during the early decades of the twentieth century, was probably best known as the biographer of Jackson and the editor of his correspondence. Thoroughly familiar with the sources available to him, Bassett's scholarly life of Old Hickory remains a highly reliable guide, and his chapter on Jackson's personal characteristics, reproduced below, is one of the most revealing portraits in print. A comparison of Bassett and Parton reveals the influence of the Progressive movement upon American historians. To Bassett, Jackson was, in spite of his limitations, a great leader of the democratic movement.*

Personal Characteristics of Andrew Jackson

Conclusion

At this point we turn from Jackson's conflicts and problems and consider the man himself. His enemies hated him and rarely saw his good qualities; his friends loved him and reluctantly admitted his failings; and in a sense each was right. Some of the good things he did are excellent and some of the bad things are wretched. His puzzling personality defies clear analysis, but we must admit that he was a remarkable man. He lacked much through the want of an education, and he acquired much through apparent accident, but it was only his strong character which turned deficiency and opportunity alike to his purpose and made his will the strongest influence in his country in his time.

The secret of his power was his adjust-ment to the period in which he lived. Other men excelled him in experience, wisdom, and balanced judgment; but the American democrats of the day admired neither of these qualities. They honored courage, strength, and directness. They could tolerate ignorance but not hesitancy. Jackson was the best embodiment of their desires from the beginning of the national government to his own day.

Jackson accepted democracy with relentless logic. Some others believed that wise leaders could best determine the policies of government, but he more than any one else of his day threw the task of judging upon the common man. And this he did without cant and in entire sincerity. No passionate dreamer of the past was more willing than he to

*John Spencer Bassett, *The Life of Andrew Jackson*, II. Garden City, N. Y.: Doubleday, Page and Co., 1911. Reprinted without footnotes by permission of Mr. Richard Bassett.

test his principles to the uttermost. "You know I never despair," he said; "I have confidence in the virtue and good sense of the people. God is just, and while we act faithfully to the Constitution, He will smile upon and prosper our exertions."

Mere military glory will (not) explain his hold on the nation. It undoubtedly had much to do with his introduction into national politics, but it soon gave place to a popularity resting on other qualities. In fact, his peculiar character shone behind his military fame and recommended him to the people. They liked his promptness in invading Florida in 1818 and his abrupt bridling of the dallying [Don José] Callava [Spanish governor of Pensacola] in 1821 as much as his victory at New Orleans. Other generals won victories in the war, but they did not become political forces through them. To the people the old government seemed weak and unequal, and Jackson, the man who solved difficulties, was elected to reform it. When the process of reform began his capacity as a political leader showed itself. Probably he could have been reëlected in 1832 independently of his war record.

Much has been said about his honesty. The historical critic and the moralist know this for a common virtue. Most of Jackson's contemporaries were as honest as he, but he excelled them in candor, which is frequently pronounced honesty. He was apt to speak his mind clearly, although he could on occasion, as has been seen, be as diplomatic as a delicate case demanded. Van Buren said in apparent sincerity that he believed "an honester or in any sense a better man was never placed at the head of the Government."

Many citations and incidents ... witness Jackson's lack of restraint and fair judgment. They seem to suggest habitual errors of mind; but we are assured that such was not the case. Even Calhoun, in the bitterness of the final quarrel, admitted that in ordinary matters and when not irritated by some unusual thing he was fair and reasonable. The explosions of anger for which he was noted were incident to a tense natural temperament; and they were apt to come when he was off his guard. In dangers which were anticipated he was extremely cool. Thus at New Orleans he broke into violent rage when he saw the column on the west bank falling back, although when the lines were assailed two hours earlier he was complete master of himself. In the long struggles against his political enemies he was never surprised into some rash explosion, although many efforts were made by opponents to lead him into such a situation. "He was," says Van Buren, "in times of peculiar difficulty and danger, calm and equable in his carriage and always master of his passions."

But Van Buren would not claim that he was fair toward an opponent. "The conciliation of individuals," he said, "formed the smallest, perhaps too small a part of his policy. His strength lay with the masses, and he knew it. He first, and at last in all public questions, always tried to be right, and when he felt that he was so he apprehended little, sometimes too little, from the opposition of prominent and powerful men, and it must now be admitted that he seldom overestimated the strength he derived from the confidence and favor of the people."

In England Van Buren came into contact with the Duke of Wellington, then a leader of the conservatives there; and he made the following comparison between the Duke and Jackson:

There were many points in which he and General Jackson resembled each other. In moral and physical courage, in indifference to personal consequences, and in promptness of action there was little if any difference in their characters. The Duke was better educated and had received the instruction of experience upon a larger scale, but the General in native intellect had, I think, been more richly endowed.

But there was a marked dissimilarity which Van Buren overlooked. The Englishman was cautious, steady, and persistent; the American was aggressive, incautious, and disposed to throw all his strength into a frontal attack. Wellington was a conservative by nature, Jackson was a radical; Wellington in politics led the party of privilege, Jackson led the party of equality. Neither could have performed the task of the other.

When Jackson became President it was expected that he would fall under the influence of favorites. His inexperience in national affairs made it essential that he should take advice freely, and he himself was conscious of it. But he was never a tool. In all his important measures he was the dominant figure. The Maysville veto was, perhaps, the affair in which another had most part, but even here Van Buren, who suggested the measure, was careful to base it on Jackson's known opposition to the invasion of state rights and to the exploitation of the public treasury by private parties. He approached the matter most cautiously and used his best tact to conceal his purpose.

Other Presidents were dependent on advice, but they usually consulted their cabinet. Jackson, when a general, rarely held military councils; when President he rarely held cabinet meetings. A formal cabinet decision limited him; he preferred to consult whom he wished, informally and without responsibility. Out of such conditions grew the "Kitchen Cabinet." This group did not control him outright; all its members approached him with great caution, and they accomplished their ends only by tact and insinuating appeals to his feelings.

If his policies were his own his documents were usually prepared by others. He was not a master of writing or argumentation, but he knew well what he would fight for. His private letters show crude reasoning to support objects which are dictated by common sense. His best documents are his military proclamations, where there is room for the play of such strong feelings as courage, endurance, and loyalty—qualities in which he was at his best.

His lack of political knowledge made him in cases where knowledge was essential a bad judge of men. In 1834 he expressed a desire to appoint Cuthbert, of Georgia, to the supreme bench, upon which Van Buren observed that there were two Cuthberts in Georgia, Alfred, of whom he had never heard that he was a lawyer, and John, whom he did not think equal to the position. Jackson took the rebuke in good spirit, and appointed another man.

Van Buren's anxiety to escape blame for participating in the removal of the [United States Bank] deposits has been alluded to; but we are hardly prepared for the following audacious utterance made the day after the order to remove went into effect:

You will see by the inclosed, that the opposition have commenced the game I anticipated. They have found by experience that their abuse of you is labour lost, and they conclude wisely that if they could succeed in shifting the Bank question from your shoulders to mine, they would be better able to serve the Mammon than they are at present. Now, although I cannot grumble at the service they are rendering me with the people, by identifying me with you in this matter, it will not do for us to expose the great measure to prejudice by doing anything that would tend in the slightest degree to withdraw from it the protection of your name.

The object of this peculiarly insidious flattery probably never suspected its nature. To the faults of a friend he was singularly blind.

Of associates other than Van Buren, [Major William B.] Lewis seems to have had influence chiefly in personal affairs. He was at home in the Eaton intrigue, the exclusion of Calhoun, and the nomination of Van Buren in 1832. He lived in the President's house and encouraged the impression that he held the key to his favor. He was able by this means to exert a wide influence among the office-seekers. Jackson used him freely in matters high and low. At one time he wants him to stay in Washington to keep an eye on the situation during the President's absence: at another he gives him all kinds of minor commissions, as writing papers and selling cotton. [Amos] Kendall had more to do with policies, but his influence came comparatively late. He was powerful in the bank controversy, a strong supporter of Jackson's anti-bank views, and after that war was won his influence survived in general matters. [Francis] Blair, who came into touch with the administration in 1830, became after a while a warm personal associate; but he was not a man of creative power. He loved Jackson and fought faithfully for him, but the many letters which passed between them show no evidence that he sought to modify the President's political life.

But Blair gave a rich friendship. He had the homely virtues of the West. His home on Pennsylvania Avenue opposite the President's house was presided over by a wife who to a larger culture added the reliable virtues of Mrs. Jackson. It was a haven of comfort to the tired spirit and body of the harassed and pain-racked Jackson, and he made touching references to it as long as he lived. To Mrs. Blair on the eve of his departure from Washington he wrote the following characteristic words:

I cannot leave this city without presenting you my grateful thanks for the great kindness you have extended to me and my family whilst here. When sick you visited us and extended to me and our dear little ones all comforts within your power. We all part with you and your dear husband and amiable family with sincere regret; but I trust in a kind providence that I may reach home and be spared until I have the pleasure of seeing you and Mr. Blair and your dear Eliza at the Hermitage. You will receive a good welcome. I beg you to accept as a memento of my regard a heifer raised by me since my second election. She will bring you in mind of my fondness for good milk, and how I was gratified in this fondness from your liberal hands.

If he had the failings of suspiciousness, narrowness, and vindictiveness, he had also the calmer virtues of domesticity and personal honor. He was peculiarly gentle with the weak. Women were pleased with his protecting chivalry. They admired his grave dignity and warm emotions. For children he had a tender heart, and the cry of an infant aroused his warm sympathy. His letters contain many expressions of pride in the developments of the children of his adopted son and of distress over their suffering. Into his relations with his relatives storms rarely entered. To them he was the clan leader and defender.

With true Southern feeling he took every woman seriously. In 1833 a New Haven spinster appealed to Van Buren to introduce her to Jackson, so that she might win his affection and become his wife. Her letter was forwarded to Jackson, who wrote in the finest possible strain, and with his own hand: "Whatever may be her virtues, I could make but one answer to any partiality they could form for me, and that is, my heart is in the grave of my dear departed wife, from which sacred spot no living being can recall it. In the cultivation of the sentiments of friendship, which are perhaps rendered more active by the loss I have sustained, I trust I shall always be able to produce suitable returns for the favor of my acquaintances; and if therefore I ever meet this lady I shall hope to satisfy her that I appreciate as I ought her kindness, tho' I cannot for a moment entertain the proposition it has led her to make."

Much of the affection of his old age centered in the family and person of his adopted son, a man whose business failures brought much sorrow. For the son's wife, Sarah York Jackson, the father had a strong affection which was well deserved by her calm and faithful care of his old age. His fatherly instinct was marked. It appears with many other virtues, in the following letter to Andrew Jackson, Jr., written from Washington, March 9, 1834, after paying many of the young man's debts:

My dear son, I recd yesterday your letter of the 16th ultimo, and have read with attention, and am more than pleased that you have taken a just view of that fatherly advice I have been constantly pressing upon you, believing as I do, that unless you adopt them you cannot possibly get well thro life and provide for an increasing family which it is now your duty to do, and have the means of giving them such education as your duty to them as a parent requires, and their standing in society, merits.

My dear son, It is enough for me that you acknowledge your error, it is the error of youth and inexperience, and my son I fully forgive them. You have my advice, it is that of a tender and affectionate father given to you for your benefit and that of your dear and amiable family, and I pray you to adhere to it in all respects and it will give peace and plenty thro life and that of your amiable Sarah and her dear little ones. Keep clear of Banks and indebtedness, and you live a freeman, and die in independence and leave your family so.

Before this reaches you, you will have received my letter enclosing Mr. Hubbs note, cancelled; and as soon as you furnish me with the full amount of the debts due by the farm, with any you may have contracted in Tennessee, and the contract with Mr. Hill for the land purchased, I will, if my means are equal to the object, free you from debt and the farm, when the farm with the aid of your own industry and economy must support us, and after I am gone, you and your family. Hence it is, and was, that I was and am so solicitous to be furnished with the full information on all the points required of you. Those who do not settle all their accounts at the end of the year, cannot know what means he really possesses, for the next; and remember, my son, that honesty and justice to all men require that we should always live within our own means, and not on those of others, when it may be, that those to whom we are indebted are relying on what we owe them, for their own support. Therefore it is unjust to live on any but our own means honestly and justly acquired. Follow this rule and a wise and just providence will smile upon your honest endeavours, and surround you with plenty, so long as you deserve it by your just and charitable conduct to all others.

In 1829 many persons thought that a democratic President would rob the office of its dignity. Their fears were only partially realized; for although the new party gave a touch of crudeness to life in Washington generally, the manners of the democratic President on formal occasions were all that could be desired. Francis Lieber, who visited him, spoke admiringly of his "noble, expressive countenance," and said: "He has the appearance of a venerable old man, his features by no means plain; on the contrary, he made the best impression on me."

Tyrone Power, the [British] actor, gives this account:

As viewed on horseback, the General is a fine, soldierly, well-preserved old gentleman, with a pale, wrinkled countenance, and a keen clear eye, restless and searching. His seat is an uncommonly good one, his hand apparently light, and his carriage easy and horseman-like; circumstances though trifling in themselves, not so general here as to escape observation. . . . Both the wife and sister of an English officer of high rank, themselves women of remarkable refinement of mind and manners, observed to me, in speaking of the President, that they had seldom met a person possessed of more native courtesy, or a more dignified deportment.

A more critical and less friendly observer was Nathaniel Sargent, who said: "In any promiscuous assembly of a thousand men he would have been pointed out above all the others as a man 'born to command,' and who would, in any dangerous emergency, be at once placed in command. Ordinarily, he had the peculiar, rough, independent, free and easy ways of the backwoodsman; but at the same time he had, whenever occasion required, and especially when in the society of ladies, very urbane and graceful manners."

John Fairfield, congressman from Maine, said of him: "He is a warmhearted, honest old man as ever lived, and possesses talents too of the first order, notwithstanding what many of our Northern folk think of him. He talks about all matters freely and fearlessly without any disguise, and in a straightforward honesty and simplicity of style and manner which you would expect from what I have before said of him. I wish some of our good folks North could hear him talk upon a subject in which he is interested, say the French question, which he talked about on Monday evening. I think their opinions would undergo a change."

Life in the President's house now lost something of the good form of the Virginia régime, but it lost nothing of the air of domesticity. Throughout most of the two administrations the household was directed by Mrs. A. J. Donelson, a woman of firm and refined character whom the people of Washington greatly respected. Her husband, a private secretary of more than ordinary ability, was related to Mrs. Jackson. Their presence in the White House gave something of the "Hermitage" feeling to the place. Politicians came and went as freely in office hours as in any exterior public office in the city. Intimates like Van Buren, Eaton, and Blair dropped in at any time, before breakfast, or in the evening, as inclination prompted; and the industrious Lewis for a large part of the administrations lived in the house. Ordinarily the President and his family made one group in the evenings. If a cabinet member, or other official, appeared to talk about public business, he read his documents or otherwise consulted with Jackson in one part of the room, the ladies sewing or chatting and the children playing meanwhile in another part.

The levees were as republican as Jefferson could wish. George Bancroft thus describes one he attended in 1831:

The old man stood in the centre of a little circle, about large enough for a cotillion, and shook hands with everybody that offered. The number of ladies who attended was small; nor were they brilliant. But to compensate for it there was a throng of apprentices, boys of all ages, men not civilized enough to walk about the room with their hats off; the vilest promiscuous medley that ever was congregated in a decent house; many of the lowest gathering round the doors, pouncing with avidity upon the wine and refreshments, tearing the cake with the ravenous keenness of intense hunger; starvelings, and fellows with dirty faces and dirty manners; all the refuse that Washington could turn forth from its workshops and stables. In one part of the room it became necessary to use a rattan.

Bancroft was ever a precise gentleman and in his own day in the capital his entertainments were models of propriety, but we cannot doubt that the people at the levee he attended were absolutely rude. Fortunately he was at a select reception and his impressions of it were better. "The old gentleman," he said, "received us as civilly as any private individual could have done; he had me introduced to all the ladies of the family, and such was the perfect ease and good breeding that prevailed there, they talked to me as though I had been an acquaintance of ten years' standing. . . . I received a very favorable impression of the President's personal character; I gave him credit for great firmness in his attachments, for sincere kindness of heart, for a great deal of philanthropy and genuine good feeling; but touching his qualifications for President, avast there—Sparta hath many a wiser than he.". . .

As his administration progressed Jackson became deeply engrossed in its controversies. Visitors were liable to have from him hot outbursts of wrath against Biddle, Clay, or Calhoun. His particular friends learned to ignore such displays, but other persons found them disagreeable. A caller who alluded to contemporary politics might have a harangue on the decay of liberty. It soon dawned on the public that the President was feeling the effects of the strain on him. Victor as he was, sorrow pressed him down, and he was much alone. Defiantly he watched his beaten foes, who dared not renew the battle as long as he was in power.

The two terms of the presidency brought him continued ill health. Chronic indigestion made it necessary to diet strictly, and but for an iron will he could hardly have lived through the period. Beside this, he suffered continually from the wounds he received in the [Jesse and Thomas Hart] Benton and [Charles] Dickinson duels. For his most distressing attacks his favorite remedy was bleeding, and he insisted on using it even when he could ill afford the weakening effects. The winter of 1832–33 was very trying; and in the following spring and summer its difficulties were increased by the death of [John] Overton and [General John] Coffee, two of his oldest and best loved friends. More than this, the period saw the culmination of the nullification movement and the opening of the controversy over the removal of the deposits. Together they brought great depression. "I want relaxation from business, and rest," he said, "but where can I get rest? I fear not on this earth." Of Coffee's death he said: "I mourn his loss with the feelings of David for his son [*sic*] Jonathan. It is useless to mourn. He is gone the way of all the earth and I will soon follow him. Peace to his manes."

It was May 6th of this year that Robert B. Randolph, a lieutenant of the navy, discharged for irregularities in his accounts, assaulted Jackson in the cabin of a steamboat at the Alexandria dock. Randolph felt aggrieved for some words in the President's letter approving the dismissal. He found the object of his wrath seated at a table; and when Jackson, who did not know him, rose, Randolph thrust out his hand with the intention, as he later asserted, of pulling the President's nose. Bystanders interfered and bore the irate lieutenant to the shore. Newspapers of both parties deplored the affair. Jackson saw in it a plot to humiliate him and believed that Duff Green [the pro-Calhoun editor of the *United States Telegraph*] was privy to it. The affair brought from him an outburst of his oldtime indignation which he expressed in the following words to Van Buren:

If this had been done [i.e., if he had been told that Randolph approached], I would have been prepared and upon my feet, when he never would have moved with life from his tracks he stood in. Still more do I regret that when I got to my feet, and extricated from the bunks, and tables, that my friends interposed, closed the passage to the door, and held me, until I was obliged to tell them if they did not open a passage I would open it with my cane. In the meantime, the villain, surrounded by his friends, had got out of the boat, crying they were carrying him to the civil authority. Thus again I was halted at the warf. Solomon says, "there's a time for all things under the sun," and if the dastard will only present himself to me, I will freely pardon him, after the interview, for every act or thing done to me, or he may thereafter do to me.

This interview, so interestingly conceived, was never brought into reality.

The protest of Southerners in 1835 against circulating abolition literature in the South also was a disturbing factor. Kendall, since 1835, postmaster-general, was asked to exclude such matter from the mails on the ground that it was incendiary: he dared not arouse the North by complying. His decision was in the spirit of the Missouri Compromise, which gave each section what it asked within its own limits. He decided that abolition literature might be mailed in the North

but need not be delivered in the South. Jackson seems to have taken little interest in the compromise, but it affected him politically. The extreme Southerners, most of them followers of Calhoun, held meetings which could have no other object than to commit the Southern people to resentment. No man in Southern politics dared oppose the meetings; for to urge that the abolitionists be tolerated was political suicide in that section. The bolder of the leaders went so far as to say that Jackson was blamable because he let this menace develop in the nation.

Jackson deprecated the alarm of the South and thought that the agitation there was unwise, not only because it imperiled his own policies through party dissension, but also because it threatened disunion. John Randolph [of Roanoke], old but undiminished in his opposition to Calhoun, realized how much Jackson meant for the preservation of nationality. "I can compare him to nothing," said the Virginian in his last illness, "but a sticking-plaster. As soon as he leaves the Government all the impurities existing in the country will cause a disruption, but while he sticks the union will last."

In 1836 the forces of sectionalism were not strong enough to affect the elections. Neither did Clay, Jackson's arch foe, feel strong enough to defeat him. He withheld his hand and trusted those democrats who objected to the elevation of Van Buren to produce enough disorganization to defeat the favorite. The defection showed first in Tennessee, where Van Buren was identified with the friends of Eaton and Lewis. Both these men were unpopular in the state, and Eaton's foes formed an efficient organization when, under [Felix] Grundy's able leadership, they defeated his hopes of the senate in 1833. Governor [William] Carroll gave the New Yorker fair warning that if he wished the state he should conciliate Grundy.

The threatened disruption took shape in December, 1834, when a majority of the Tennessee members of the national house of representatives endorsed Judge [Hugh Lawson] White for President. Jackson was so greatly surprised at this evidence of division that he refused at first to believe his old friend would forsake him. Other states followed the lead of Tennessee. White's boom seemed propitiously launched, but it gained no force in the North and Northwest, where it was not desired to see another Tennessee President. [William Henry] Harrison, of Indiana, and Webster got endorsement in their respective sections, and the opponents of Van Buren began to nope they could throw the election into the house. But they could not shake the hold of the strong machine which the Jackson managers had built up. The results showed 170 votes for Van Buren and 124 for all his opponents. It was a party triumph, but with it was a drop of bitterness: Tennessee went for White and with it went Georgia, on which Jackson lavished all his care in the matter of the Cherokees [and their removal from the state]. Harrison's vote was chiefly in the Northwest and Webster's in New England. South Carolina threw her vote away on [Willie P.] Mangum, a Southern whig, but the Jackson organization maintained its hold on North Carolina, Virginia, Pennsylvania, and New York, all old republican states, who together cast 110 of the 148 electoral votes necessary to a choice.

From the election in November events hurried on to the meeting of congress in December. The last annual message, December 5th, was in a tone of triumph. Of the issues before the country in 1829, all had been settled to Jackson's satisfaction. Internal improvements were relegated to the background, the tariff was compromised and the "American system" was checked, the Bank of the United States was closing up its affairs, nullification was laid low, foreign affairs were on a satisfactory basis and our prestige was heightened, the national debt was discharged and revenues were abundant beyond expectation, the irritating situation in Georgia was pacified, and above all the party organization was established on a splendid popular basis. This totality of achievement was so great that it was hardly discredited by the anxiety that came from the Mexican situation and from the uncertain state of the currency. The panic of the following year was not yet discernible. The message closed with an expression of gratitude "to the great body of my fellow-citizens, in whose partiality and indulgence I have found encouragement and support in many difficult and trying scenes through which it has been my lot to pass during my political career.... All that has occurred during my administration is calculated to inspire me with increased confidence in the stability of our institutions."

When this message was written he had taken steps for a more formal farewell. The idea was in his mind in 1831, before he decided to stand for reëlection. He recurred to it in 1836, and October 13th wrote to [Roger B.] Taney, now his chief agent in preparing such papers, asking for assistance. The subjects he wished to treat, he said, were the glorious union and the schemes of dissatisfied men to dissolve it, the drift toward monopolies, the attempts to "adulterate the currency" with paper money, the rage for speculation and stock-jobbing, and all other things which tended to corrupt the simple virtue which was left us by the fathers. The danger he foresaw for the spirit of union especially alarmed him. "How to impress the public," he said, "with an adequate aversion to the sectional jealousies, the sectional parties, and sectional preferences which centring on mischievous and intriguing individuals, give them power to disturb and shake our happy confederacy, is a matter which has occupied my own thought greatly." He asked Taney to "throw on paper" his ideas on these subjects. Taney willingly complied and promised to bring the result with him when he came to Washington about New Year's to open the regular term of the supreme court. The *Farewell Address,* issued March 4, 1837, follows closely the copy which is preserved in Taney's handwriting in the Jackson manuscripts.

The whigs declared it presumptuous and self-conceited for this ignorant old man, as they called him, to send out a farewell address in imitation of Washington. The extravagance of their criticism discredited their argument and, as in other cases, brought sympathy to its object. Jackson as the leader of a great party might with propriety assume to give them advice. But his advice in itself was not remarkable. The appeal for union was well conceived, but it was overcast by the other points in the document, points which were after all but the re-stated argument of a thousand democratic stumps in the preceding campaign. But the address pleased the democrats, and many a copy on white satin was laid away as a valuable memento of the time.

Ere the people of Washington read the address they crowded the famous "Avenue" to see its author, pale and trembling from disease, ride up to the place at which he laid down his office. The scene gratified his soul. The oath was administered by Chief Justice Taney, twice rejected by the senate but now in office through an awakening of popular opinion: it was taken by Van Buren, who also had been made to feel the effects of the senate's ire. The plaudits of the great multitude were chiefly for the outgoing President. The polite and unruffled Van Buren aroused little enthusiasm; but the frank, convinced, and hardhitting man at his side had either the love or the hatred of men. For weeks before his exit from office he was overwhelmed by visitors, delegations, and addresses from organizations to express approval of his course and good will for his future. When he left Washington on March 7th, his journey was impeded by the demonstrations of his friends. Eighteen days later he arrived in Nashville.

Writing to his successor he characterized his term of office as follows: "The approbation I have received from the people everywhere on my return home on the close of my official life, has been a source of much gratification to me. I have been met at every point by numerous democratic–republican friends, and many repenting whigs, with a hearty welcome and expressions of 'well done thou faithful servant.' This is truly the patriot's reward, the summit of my gratification, and will be my solace to my grave. When I review the arduous administration through which I have passed, the formidable opposition, to its very close, of the combined talents, wealth and power of the whole aristocracy of the United States, aided as it is, by the monied monopolies of the whole country with their corrupting influence, with which we had to contend, I am truly thankful to my God for this happy result. . . . It displays the virtue and power of the sovereign people, and that all must bow to their will. But it was the voice of this sovereign will that so nobly sustained us against this formidable power and enabled me to pass through my administration so as to meet its approbation." No words of the author could characterize Jackson better than these from his own pen. They give a sincere and faithful explanation of his inner self, and they are unconscious of their own egotism.

*   *   *   *

... Time has softened some of the asperities of the epoch in which he lived. The American who now knows how to estimate the life of the Jacksonian era will take something from the pretensions of his enemies and add something to the virtues hitherto accorded his partisans. Jackson's lack of education, his crude judgments in many affairs, his occasional outbreaks of passion, his habitual hatred of those enemies with whom he had not made friends for party purposes, and his crude ideas of some political policies—all lose some of their infelicity in the face of his brave, frank, masterly leadership of the democratic movement which then established itself in our life. This was his task: he was adapted to it; he did it faithfully, conscientiously, ably. Few American Presidents have better lived up to the demands of the movement which brought them into power.

VERNON L. PARRINGTON (1871-1929),
Kansas-born Populist and Harvard Ph.D. in English,
wrote one of the most provocative books in American
intellectual history, *Main Currents in American
Thought.* A Jeffersonian liberal, he found a
fundamental ideological conflict in American history
between the spirit of the Declaration of Independence
and the Constitution, the one devoted to the rights
of man and the other to the rights of property, the
one looking to Jefferson and the other to Hamilton.
Writing as a disillusioned Progressive in
the 1920s, Parrington viewed the end result of
Jacksonianism as a rejection of Jeffersonian liberalism,
which for him constituted one of the central
tragedies of American history.*

Andrew Jackson, Agrarian Liberal

The dramatic career of Andrew Jackson, so unlike that of Jefferson, which was determined by a speculative temperament and founded on a critical examination of diverse systems of society and politics, was shaped in large measure by prejudice and circumstance. A man of iron will and inflexible purpose, he was almost wholly lacking in political and social philosophy. His conclusions were the reactions of a simple nature of complete integrity, in contact with plain fact. Fundamentally realistic, he cherished few romanticisms. There was no subtlety in his mental processes and this lack kept him free from the temptation to follow devious paths beloved of politicians. He must take the shortest way to his objective, crashing through such obstacles as lay in his path. He was never a bookish man. He was surprisingly ill read, and his grammar and spelling were those of the plain people. He loved horse racing and was a master of profanity; yet in spite of characteristics that link him with Davy Crockett, he possessed an innate dignity and chivalry that set him far above the wag of the canebrakes. He was a born leader whose headlong onslaughts and rash mistakes might imperil the cause but could not shake the confidence of his followers. All who knew a man when they saw one respected Andrew Jackson. Imperious and dictatorial, he knew how to command but not to obey; he took orders

*From *The Romantic Revolution* in America by Vernon L. Parrington, copyright 1927, by Harcourt, Brace & World, Inc.; renewed, 1954, by Vernon L. Parrington, Jr., Louise P. Tucker, and Elizabeth P. Thomas. Reprinted by permission of the publishers.

from no one, not even his superiors, unless such orders fell in with his own plans. In short General Jackson represented the best which the new West could breed in the way of capable and self reliant individualism, and the backwoodsmen loved him for the enemies he made, and backed him loudly in his fight against the aristocratic East.

When Jackson settled in Nashville in 1788, at the age of twenty-one, the Cumberland valley had somewhat under five thousand inhabitants scattered a distance of eighty-five miles along the river. The first settlements had been made only nine years before, and Nashville was a frontier post with frontier manners. Into this rough society the young Scotch-Irishman fitted easily. His smattering of the law sufficed to gain him clients and he soon became a local political leader. When he was only twenty-nine he was sent to Philadelphia as the first Congressman from the state of Tennessee, where he came in contact with the "aristocratic Neebobs" of the government and heartily disliked them. The next year he was sent to the Senate, but a single session satisfied him and he resigned to accept a judgeship in the state Supreme Court, which post he held for six years. During these early years he was unconsciously following the path that conducted straight to a middle-class philosophy. He threw himself into speculation, bought and sold land in great blocks, traded in horses and slaves, set up a general store, and was well on the road to wealth when the panic of 1795 caught him unprepared. He lost most of his extensive holdings, including his homestead and many of his slaves, and removed to a six hundred and forty acre tract eight miles from Nashville—the Hermitage—which was to become one of the famous places of America. With this removal

his middle-class ambitions fell away and he became a planter with a simple agrarian point of view; and this old-fashioned agrarianism became in later years the determining force in all his political thinking.

He was fifty-eight when he emerged as a potential candidate for the Presidency in 1822, and for years his sole interests, other than those of his plantation, had been military. He was singularly wanting in any formulated political philosophy, and his reëlection to the Senate two years later did little to supply the lack. He had picked up some shreds of the protectionist theory and in a letter written in 1824 he went so far as to declare for a "judicious" protective tariff, basing his view on the grounds of the country's economic unpreparedness at the time of the War of 1812, on the lack of markets for the produce of western farms, and on the desirability of drawing labor from the farm to the factory. But he added a significant passage that reveals the agrarian bias of his mind. To the end of his life he insisted that he was an old Republican of 1798, and this comment of 1824 suffices to connect his later attack on the Bank with Jefferson's attack on Hamilton's fiscal policy.

Beyond this, I look at the Tariff with an eye to the proper distribution of labor and revenue; and with a view to discharge our national debt. I am one of those who do not believe that a national debt is a national blessing, but rather a curse to a republic; inasmuch as it is calculated to raise around the administration a moneyed aristocracy dangerous to the liberties of the country. (Quoted in Bassett, *Life of Andrew Jackson*, Vol. I, p. 346.)

The tariff was the only question on which he was receptive to Whiggish arguments, and although he never openly repudiated a protectionist policy he soon grew lukewarm in its support. Such other fragments of Whiggery as found accidental lodgment in his mind were swept away in the fierce struggles that marked his years in the White House. During those eight years Jackson found himself, and the man who emerged from the struggle was an agrarian of the old Virginian school. As he came to understand the significance of the principle of exploitation he learned to interpret social classes in terms of economics. He instinctively hated all aristocrats, extending his dislike to the circle that pretended to social preëminence in Tennessee, speaking of them contemptuously as the "aristocrats of Nashville." But in these later years a change in his vocabulary appeared; his favorite phrases became "the monied capitalists" and the "hydra of corruption." He had come to associate aristocracy with the control of the economics of society. He was learning how aristocracies are built up through the instrumentality of the state; and as that lesson sank into his mind his opposition to such class favoritism hardened into adamant. He would put a stop to such practices, cost what it might. His attack on the Bank was perhaps the most courageous act in our political history; he knew how fiercely it would be defended; yet he was amazed at the number of hornets that issued from the shaken nest. "Such has been the scenes of corruption in our last congress," he wrote in 1833, "that I loath the corruption of human nature and long for retirement, and repose on the Hermitage. But until I can strangle this hydra of corruption, the Bank, I will not shrink from my duty." And a little later, "I want relaxation from business and rest, but where can I get rest; I fear not on this earth" (Bassett, *Life of Andrew Jackson*, Vol. II, pp. 635, 637).

As his policy unfolded it became clear that Jackson had not changed with the changing times. He remained to the last the product of an earlier domestic economy, with an old-fashioned horror of debt. He was too generous to be frugal, too kind-hearted to be thrifty, too honest to live above his means. He desired a simple independence for himself and for his country. He believed that the government should pay its debt, reduce its revenues, and live simply. In his austere personal rectitude he exhibited a Puritan conviction of the sacredness of stewardship; he must return to the common people, who had put their trust in him, an honest reckoning of that trust. It was not in his nature to betray their faith. He would have nothing to do with the new theory that government is an agency to help business. To take profits from an instrument erected supposedly for the common good was abhorrent to his old-fashioned views; it was impossible for him to lend the sanction of his office to particular or special interests; and when circumstances made the Bank the central vexing problem of his administration, his position was predetermined by every conviction of his mind. While he was President he would not allow the government to be used for business ends; he would not permit its funds or credit to be turned to private profits; he would not tolerate a money monopoly, no matter how conventionally correct its operations might be proved to be, that challenged the sovereignty of the national government. The twin powers of the purse and sword—to recall Clay's famous phrase that every Whig orator used on the stump—were in Jackson's opinion the ultimate tests of sovereignty; and to turn over the money of the government to private hands for private use, he believed, was as grave an abrogation of sovereign rights as would be the use of the army and navy by private interests for private ends.

In the judgment of many critics Jackson, in his ignorance of the intricacies of capitalistic finance, wantonly destroyed a necessary credit system, thereby bringing a devastating panic on the country. Whether or not that judgment is true is of little importance today. More interesting historically is the fact that in his attitude towards the Bank, as in his attitude towards internal improvements, Jackson returned to the agrarian position of Jefferson and John Taylor, nullifying for a time the victories gained by the middle class during the boom period of nationalism. The more he learned about the methods of capitalistic finance, the more he distrusted it. His prejudices were his strength. He disliked speculation and he could see nothing permanently wise or sound in a speculative economy that put American industry at the mercy of bankers to expand or contract credit. With an old-fashioned love of a stable currency he gave his warm support to the project to return the country to a specie basis. "The great desideratum, in modern times," he said in his message to the twenty-fourth Congress, "is an efficient check upon the power of banks, preventing that excessive issue of paper whence arise those fluctuations in the standard of value which render uncertain the rewards of labor." The establishment of additional mints to provide an adequate coinage of gold or silver became therefore a natural corollary of his attack upon bank currency. It was John Taylor's economics written into the law of the land.

In his attitude towards the state Jackson followed the nationalistic tendencies of the West. He was as patriotic as Clay, and in spite of strong states-rights sym-

pathies he contemptuously rejected Calhoun's theory of nullification. But he had no love for an omnicompetent state. More and more he drifted back to the Jeffersonian position in his conception of the powers and duties of the federal government. Replying to the vote of censure of 1834, he stated his ideal of government in words that would have become Jefferson's first inaugural speech. He had been charged with being ambitious, to which he replied:

> The ambition which leads me on, is an anxious desire and a fixed determination, to return to the people, unimpaired, the sacred trust they have confided to my charge —to heal the wounds of the constitution and preserve it from further violation; to persuade my countrymen, so far as I may, that it is not in a splendid government, supported by powerful monopolies and aristocratical establishments, that they will find happiness, or their liberties protected, but in a plain system, void of pomp—protecting all, and granting favors to none—dispensing its blessings like the dews of heaven, unseen and unfelt, save in the freshness and beauty they contribute to produce. It is such a government that the genius of our people requires—such a one only under which our States may remain for ages to come, united, prosperous, and free. (Benton, *Thirty Years' View*, Vol. I, p. 427.)

The evils entailed on America by the Jacksonian revolution were many, but they cannot properly be charged against Andrew Jackson. They came in spite of him, and they came as a result of the great object lesson in the manipulation of the majority will that his popularity had laid bare. His instincts and the main outline of his policy were Jeffersonian; but neither he nor any other man was strong enough to stop the current of middle-class individualism then running. The American people were wanting in an adequate democratic program suited to the changing times, as they were wanting in desire for a social democracy. And when his capable hands fell from the machine he had created, it was seized by the politicians and used for narrow partisan ends. Yet one far-reaching result survived the movement, the popularization of the name of democracy and the naïve acceptance of the belief that the genius of America was democratic. In choosing a party name the Jacksonians were shrewder politicians and better prophets than the Whigs. For better or worse the American masses, and in particular the nationalistic West, had espoused the principle of democracy, and interpreted it in terms of political equalitarianism—a principle that had inspired a fanatical hatred in the breasts of old Federalists. To gentlemen of that earlier school democracy had meant the right of the propertyless majority to plunder the minority in the name of the law. The later Whigs did not make so blundering a mistake. Instead of proclaiming

democracy the mother of all mischiefs, they welcomed it as an effective aid in vote-getting. Learning their lesson from Jackson, the Whig politicians outdid him in democratic professions. They had discovered that business has little to fear from a skillfully guided electorate; that quite the safest way, indeed, to reach into the public purse is to do it in the sacred name of the majority will. Perhaps the rarest bit of irony in American history is the later custodianship of democracy by the middle class, who while perfecting their tariffs and subsidies, legislating from the bench, exploiting the state and outlawing all political theories but their own, denounce all class consciousness as unpatriotic and all agrarian or proletarian programs as undemocratic. But it was no fault of Andrew Jackson if the final outcome of the great movement of Jacksonian democracy was so untoward; it was rather the fault of the times that were not ripe for democracy.

CLAUDE G. BOWERS (1879-1958), journalist, biographer, diplomat, and historian, finds the central theme of American history in a struggle between the forces of democracy and aristocracy. The vivid and dramatic style that characterizes his studies of the Jeffersonians and Jacksonians assures widespread familiarity with and interest in his books. Jefferson and Jackson emerge as master political leaders, formulators and guardians of the democratic tradition and opponents of privilege. In fact, interpreted through the skilful pen and oratory of Bowers, the main lines of American History appear as the working out of the goals of the Democratic party. His optimism contrasts strongly with the pessimism of his fellow liberal, Parrington, both of whom published in the 1920s.*

Andrew Jackson: The Homeric Battles of His Administration

I

When in the election of 1828 Andrew Jackson was borne on the backs of the people to the seat of power, a new day dawned in American history. The democratic philosophy of Thomas Jefferson became a reality. That ideology of liberty and personal rights to which Jefferson arrived through study and meditation was inherent in the nature of his disciple. In the wilderness among the pioneers, in the camps from which robust individualists and patriots followed him to victories, among the valiant men who cleared the forests and plowed the fields, he had lived the democracy he felt. From these associations had come his contempt for show and sham and snobbery, his distrust of the too great centralization of power, his hostility to monopoly, his challenge to the growing influence of wealth and privilege, and his utter devotion to the interest of the common man.

Jackson was the first of the Presidents to fight his way from actual poverty to power. His parents had migrated to America from Ireland to escape oppression and in search of opportunity. The death of his father in his fourteenth year left him wholly dependent on his own resources. At that early age when the patriots of the colonies began their march to independence, he joined the Revolutionary army. He saw his brothers

---

* From Claude G. Bowers, *Making Democracy A Reality: Jefferson, Jackson, and Polk*. Memphis: Memphis State College Press, 1954.

39

fall in the fight for freedom, and sorrow killed his mother. Taken prisoner, he was struck down by the saber of a Hessian officer whose boots he had refused to polish. He was to have his revenge at New Orleans in 1815. . . .

II

Who was Jackson, the man whose historic battles made democracy a reality? . . . Once convinced that he was right, he faced his foes, if need be, singlehanded. He was an intense individualist, subordinate to no man, dependent on no man's support. Some one has said that "the wolves hunt in packs, but the lion hunts alone." We have the real Jackson on the occasion at the Capitol when an assassination was attempted, and the frail old man, with uplifted cane, advanced on the assassin who held the smoking pistol in his hand. . . .

Perhaps it is not beneath the dignity of history to recall how he impressed one stranger who called at the White House. On leaving he told a friend that he had never met such a courtly and polished gentleman. A bit surprised, the friend replied that Old Hickory was a great soldier and statesman, but how, he asked, had the visitor found polish. "Well," was the answer, "he asked me if I would have a nip of whiskey. I told him I would not mind. He went out and came back with a jug of whiskey and a glass and handed them to me. Then he went to the window looking out, with his back to me, while I poured."

His honesty was proverbial. Not least among the reasons for the people's faith in him was his unimpeachable integrity. When in his earlier days he endorsed a note for a friend who did not honor it,

he did not doubt his duty. He sold his first home in Tennessee with 30,000 acres to meet his obligation of honor without hesitation. It was then that he moved deeper into the country and built the log cabin he called the Hermitage, later to be replaced by the stately mansion which today is one of the nation's patriotic shrines. Such was his reputation for integrity that, when during a crisis in New Orleans, a draft of the Secretary of War was refused, Jackson was able to borrow $25,000 on his personal note without difficulty since his note was as good as gold in the bank.

That he was quick-tempered and could be violent in anger cannot be denied. He was much more high-strung than most men. But there was another side to his character—he could be as tender as a woman, and he loved children. Following a battle with the savages in which he had prevailed after a slaughter, he noticed a small Indian boy whose parents had been killed, and turning to an Indian woman he asked her to give it nourishment. "All his relatives are dead," she said. "Kill him too." Cut to the heart, he took the child under his protection and introduced him into his household where he was treated as though a son. His happiest hours in the White House were when playing with the children. A child's cry in the night would arouse him, and the old man would rise in the cold, go to the child's room, and walk the floor with it until it fell asleep. Benton has left us the story of having found him on a wet, cold evening seated alone before the fire with a child and a lamb between his knees. His passion of tenderness was as strong as that of hate. In his character is verified the words of the poet, "The bravest are the tenderest, The loving are the daring." . . .

III

The three most historic phases of the Jackson administrations were rich in drama. First, Jackson the nationalist.

Here he was engaged in a contest with John C. Calhoun. There is a background to their duel on nationalism that wrecked a friendship and probably prevented one of the greatest of Americans from reaching the presidency. Jackson had announced that he would have no one in his cabinet who had presidential aspirations. Calhoun, then Vice President, was conspicuous among the candidates; Martin Van Buren, though an aspirant, had cautiously kept his ambition undercover, and, without knowing of his aspirations, Jackson made him Secretary of State. This was resented by Calhoun though the breach then made was not too important.

The second incident had more deadly repercussions. Having heard that in the cabinet of Monroe the proposal had been made to discipline him for his action in Florida, Jackson had understood that his critic in the cabinet had been William H. Crawford. One day Jackson gave a dinner in honor of Monroe, then in retirement, and in the gossip across the table he was told that it was Calhoun who had proposed the censure. From that moment Jackson looked on Calhoun as an enemy.

These incidents had no direct connection with the savage battle with the South Carolinian which was to dramatize the Jackson administration. Up until 1816 the South Carolinians had been robust nationalists, but the tariff act of that year, in the interest of the industrialists of New England and detrimental to the economic interest of their section, aroused their ire; the tariff of 1828 was a more defiant piece of sectional legisla-

tion, and the conviction grew that the farmers of the South were to be immolated on the altar of New England greed. With the North predominant in Congress, not a few Southerners were persuaded that the ruin of the South was certain if the protective tariff policy to serve the special interest of the industrial North was to become the permanent policy of the nation

Looming high above all the other statesmen of the South was John C. Calhoun. He had begun his career as an ardent nationalist, but the tariff policy alarmed him. He was a great political scientist and philosopher, a powerful orator whose speeches had the quality of Edmund Burke's orations, and he was a true patriot. He loved the Union but was convinced that the continuance of sectional legislation would end in the disruption of the Union that he loved. Out of his meditations came his doctrine of nullification—the right of a state to treat a law enacted by Congress as a nullity.

The struggle, now inevitable, was foreshadowed in the famous debate of Webster and Hayne in which the latter enunciated the Calhoun doctrine. The nullifiers formulated a plan to popularize their theory; they would take advantage of the first Jefferson birthday dinner in Washington to demonstrate their strength. The purpose was to capitalize on the popularity of the author of the Kentucky and Virginia Resolutions of 1798, which were designed to prevent the scrapping of the Bill of Rights and the establishment of a despotism. These resolutions were designed to force debate, to arouse the people to the danger to their freedoms. But—and here is the difference—Jefferson made it clear to Madison that they were not to be used in justification of armed resistance.

Jackson was invited to the dinner to create the impression that he, too, was sympathetic toward the nullification doctrine. No one doubted that he was a champion of states' rights; that he was hostile to the protective tariff; and that he loved the South. The twenty-four toasts on the program were all in support of nullification. With his usual insight into men and motives, Jackson sensed the nature and purpose of the dinner, and he sat down with Van Buren to determine the attitude he would take should the speeches be of the nature he feared. While the conspirators were felicitating themselves on the expected presence of the President, he was discussing with Van Buren the most effective way to dramatize his dissent.

The plan made, Jackson with Van Buren repaired to the dinner. The very thought of a conspiracy that would destroy the Union had aroused the lion in him. Always high-strung, he went to the repast prepared for battle. It was Old Hickory, the fighter, who sat down at the table and awaited events. He went "with feelings akin to those which would have animated his breast if the scene of this preliminary skirmish in defense of the Union had been a field of battle instead of a festive board."

Surveying the company, he found ample justification for his fear that mischief was afoot. The toasts to be proposed left no doubt. The congressional delegation from Pennsylvania left the banquet hall before the speeches; others, fearing a misinterpretation of their presence, quietly departed. The toasts began. Jackson in his chair sat impassive and immobile, an image carved in granite, his expression stern. At length, the speeches over, he was invited to propose a toast. Van Buren, who was short, mounted a chair to note the effect upon the company. Drawing himself up to his full height, he stood for a moment in silence looking at Calhoun; and then the silence was broken with a toast that made history and has rung like a clarion call down the corridors of time: "Our Federal Union—it must be preserved!"

It was more than a toast—it was a presidential proclamation; it was more than that—it was a declaration of war on all conspiracies to break the union of the states. He had thrown a bomb. The scene lost its festive air. The conspirators stood about in groups, their jubilation gone, and Jackson, giving no indication that he had done anything unusual, sauntered to the far end of the room to engage Benton in light conversation. This was in 1830.

In his home at Fort Hill, Calhoun finished his celebrated "exposition" announcing the doctrine of nullification, and the committee in the South Carolina legislature announced it as its own. It was the year of the savage presidential election of 1832, and Jackson was home at the Hermitage when he learned that the nullifiers had won a majority of seats in the South Carolina legislature. With his mind remote from the election, he hurried back to Washington fully panoplied for battle. When his friends appeared with news of his victory at the polls, he brushed them aside with mere thanks. Then he made one comment, "The best thing about this, gentlemen, is that it strengthens my hands in this struggle."

When three days later the legislature called the nullification convention for November 3, Jackson had already made his preliminary preparations. Secretary of War [Lewis] Cass ordered additional troops to Fort Moultrie; a secret emissary had been sent to Charleston to confer with Joel Poinsett, the leader of the

Unionists there, for a report on the condition of the forts; and Poinsett was reading Jackson's words: "I am well advised as to the views and proceedings of the leading nullifiers. We are wide-awake here. The Union will be preserved; rest assured of this."

The convention met and adopted the nullification ordinance, and the legislature convened and enacted laws in conformity. While the Carolina Unionists met in convention and denounced the doctrine, Jackson sent 5,000 stands of muskets with equipment to Fort Pinckney and ordered a sloop of war with smaller vessels to the Charleston harbor.

Jackson has been called a rash and violent man, but, furious as he was, his mind was clear, his judgment just, and he took not a single step that did not meticulously accord with the Constitution and the laws. "The Union must be preserved and the laws duly executed," he wrote, "but by proper means. . . . The crisis must be met, and as far as my constitutional and legal powers authorize, will be met with energy and firmness."

Meanwhile, Jackson was at work on the proclamation he was to give the nation. He himself wrote the first draft, his pen spluttering over the paper. With Edward Livingston, who was to phrase it, he was in constant contact day and night. He was not happy. He loved his native state but thought the people wrong. He did not want to use force. One night he left his seat beside the fire where he sat puffing on his clay pipe, and going to the table on which was the picture of Rachel and her Bible, he wrote a touching appeal to the patriotism of his native state and sent it to Livingston with a note: "I submit the above as the conclusion of the Proclamation for your amendment and revision.

Let it receive your best flight of eloquence to strike to the heart, and speak to the feelings of my deluded countrymen of South Carolina."

The day the proclamation was given to the nation, Jackson was like a war charger at the sound of the bugle call. His plans were made. When he received the acts of the South Carolina legislature, he would go to Congress for legal and constitutional means to enforce the object of the proclamation. The Unionists under Poinsett were preparing to fight, but Jackson held them back.

The proclamation is a classic of American nationalism and ranks among the great state papers of history. Webster was delighted, John Marshall reassured, John Quincy Adams thought it a "blister plaster," and only Henry Clay refused his commendation. His reason is quite clear. As a perennial candidate for President he was angling for the support of the extreme states' rights men; and Van Buren was equally coy for the same reason though New York had acclaimed the proclamation with enthusiasm. Even so violent a Whig as Philip Hone was writing in his diary that it would "take its place in the archives of our country, and dwell in the memory of our citizens alongside the Farewell Address." Years later President Coolidge was to say that as a state paper the proclamation is "one of the greatest of any American President."

And now the issue had been made. Resigning the vice presidency in the crisis to take his seat in the Senate to defend his doctrine, Calhoun reached Washington. His people had crossed the Rubicon on nullification, but he had aroused them to a pitch he knew to be dangerous; many were out of control. At this juncture Jackson, moving scrupulously within the framework of the law and the Constitution, called on Congress for authority to use force if necessary. When the proclamation was given teeth by the force bill, no one longer doubted his grim determination to enforce the law and to preserve the Union.

Meanwhile, the administration forces, inspired by Jackson, had sponsored the Verplanck tariff bill drastically reducing the tariff and promising a further reduction still. He hoped to deprive the nullifiers of a weapon; most of all, he wished to prevent the spread of the nullification doctrine to other parts of the South. And here enters one of the ironies of history. Clay and the protectionists, against whose unjust tariff acts the nullifiers had arrayed themselves, were joined by the nullifiers to defeat the reduction of the tariff. When the bill had been mutilated by innumerable amendments, Jackson lost interest and the bill was dropped.

The debate on the force bill was one of the most brilliant and intense in our history since it revolved around the fundamentals. As the debate progressed, three brilliant Southern Senators championed the measure. There by the side of Jackson was Felix Grundy of Tennessee, stateman and forensic orator without a peer; William C. Rives of Virginia, statesman and diplomat, the finest type of gentleman in old Virginia; and John Forsyth of Georgia, the most powerful debater in the Senate. But Jackson was not satisfied with the course of the debate. The immortal trio, Clay, Webster, and Calhoun, had not yet spoken. He knew that from Clay nothing could be expected, and that from Calhoun would come one of his greatest and most powerful speeches. He knew that the one man qualified to cross swords with the great Carolinian was Webster. With Jackson action followed close on thought.

One day the carriage of Livingston drew up at the door of Webster's lodging. The great orator was asked to enter the debate and reply to Calhoun. More, he was invited to assume the leadership on the floor and to offer any amendments he thought fit and proper. The invitation from Jackson appealed not only to his patriotism but to his vanity, and he accepted. Had Webster maintained the relations he then enjoyed with the iron man in the White House, he might have realized his life's ambition for the presidency.

The speech of Calhoun was probably the greatest he ever made, powerful in logic, profound in philosophy, and moving in eloquence; Webster replied with one of his greatest orations, brilliant, closely reasoned, free from personalities and passion—and the final words in the great debate had been spoken.

Meanwhile, Calhoun had unleashed a force at home that threatened to go beyond his intent since he was convinced that, driven to the last resort, Jackson would strike with every weapon given him by the Constitution and the law. With a spirit of compromise hovering over the Senate, an appeal was made to Henry Clay by one of his friends, but not by Jackson, to propose a compromise on the tariff. Thus came the compromise of 1833. History should have made it clear that Clay's action was motivated less by a desire to save the Union than by his wish to save the tariff system. We need no better proof than the opening words of his speech: "I believe that the American system [the tariff] is in the greatest danger." Another Whig leader, John M. Clayton, was franker when he said he "would never surrender the tariff even to save the Union."

The Clay bill conceded less to the planters of the South than that of the administration which the nullifiers had scorned, but conditions had changed. Jackson, in the White House with legal, constitutional weapons in his hand, had sent General Winfield Scott to Charleston with instructions to repel any attack upon the forts. So, despite features of the bill that were repugnant to Calhoun, he accepted them under the duress of necessity.

He hurried back to South Carolina to urge the acceptance of the compromise and the ordinance of nullification was rescinded by a vote of 153 to 4. Jackson had killed nullification without firing a shot and saved the Union without a violation of the Constitution or the law.

It hurt him to part with old friends on an issue he thought vital; and it grieved him to be forced to action against a people of a state he loved; but looming above all else was his love of the Union he had taken a solemn oath to defend. His position was all the harder because he, too, resented a tariff policy conceived in the interest of one section to the detriment of his South. He, too, was a champion of states' rights within the Union. He, too, was shocked by the fanatic, irresponsible crusade of the abolitionists, but above all else was his love of the Union which he defended at a critical moment with all the energy and firmness of his nature while moving against its enemies, despite his fury, with a cold, calculating respect for the Constitution and the laws.

His action at this time and his proclamation to the people place him among the most militant nationalists the nation has produced. . . .

[Sections IV and V are omitted. Bowers maintains that Jackson's foreign policy was highly successful and gives him credit for raising the prestige of the nation to a new height—which it has retained and which will continue "so long as the spirit of Old Hickory inspires our conduct in international affairs."]

VI

As a nationalist Jackson had succeeded in preserving the Union. In the international field he had successfully served notice that the nation would fight, if need be, for the prestige and dignity of the republic. Yet, in a third field came his greatest service—his Homeric battles for the preservation of our democratic institutions and the subordination of money to men in the determination of national policies. Here his struggle was with the Bank of the United States.

This bank was born of the brain of Alexander Hamilton who despised democracy and sincerely believed that organized wealth should dominate the government and that governmental stability is assured when government is made a source of revenue to the powerful. Thomas Jefferson foresaw its ultimate effect and opposed its establishment. When it was created, Jefferson wrote Monroe that "we are completely saddled and bridled, and the bank is so firmly mounted on us that we must go where they will guide us." In a letter to Albert Gallatin ten years later, he wrote that from the character of the bank directors and their sentiments and from their press he knew the direction they were going: "Now while we are strong it is the greatest debt we owe to the safety of our Constitution to bring this powerful enemy to a perfect subordination under its authority." And that same year in a letter to John W. Eppes he wrote, "This bank oligarchy or monarchy enters the field with ninety million dollars to direct and control the politics of the nation; and of the influence on our politics, and into what scale it will be thrown we have abundant experience."

Andrew Jackson was an ardent follower of Thomas Jefferson when the bank was created by a narrow congressional majority. He believed, as Jefferson believed, that it was unconstitutional; and, like Jefferson, he knew that it would use its power through its control of credit and the liberal use of money to dominate the politics of the nation. Jefferson never altered his opinion, and neither did Jackson.

When Jackson assumed the presidency this moneyed institution, conscious of its power, had reached the height of its arrogance and condescension. The existing charter of the bank had five years to run. The issue was not immediate nor acute. The majority of the cabinet was not unfriendly to the bank; and the majority never were to be militant supporters of the bank policy of their chief. But close to Jackson were Amos Kendall and Francis Blair of the much-maligned Kitchen Cabinet of practical politicians, and these were uncompromising enemies of the institution.

It is not remarkable that in his message to Congress in December, 1830, Jackson should have questioned the constitutionality of the bank. In its original form it was a slashing attack. After its completion it was submitted for criticism to James A. Hamilton. In him we have one of the mysteries of history. He was the son of Alexander Hamilton, the creator of the bank, but he had renounced the Federalist party and had warmly aligned himself with its enemies. When he returned the message to Jackson, the reference to the bank was in a brief paragraph questioning its constitutionality and asserting that it had "failed in the great end of establishing a uniform and sound currency." Jackson accepted the

change. However, word had trickled out that the message would be an attack, and some administration papers launched vigorous attacks upon it. But with the existing charter running for five years, there was a pause. In his message of December, 1831, Jackson merely referred to his observations in the previous message.

Meanwhile, Nicholas Biddle, the president of the bank, alarmed by the gossip, was writing his friends that the reference to the bank in the message was merely the personal view of Jackson without the support of the cabinet, and that it had not even been accepted as the position of Jackson's party. At this time Henry Clay was assuring Biddle that Jackson not only would not veto a rechartering of the bank five years before the expiration of the old charter, but would sign a recharter bill. Biddle, however, found his anxiety increasing when the vultures of politics began descending upon him with demands for money. Duff Green of the Washington *Telegraph* had applied for a loan of $20,000. It was at this time that Biddle began an assiduous cultivation of the press with the money of the bank, the government deposits.

After the second message Clay began to urge on Biddle an immediate application for a recharter, five years before the expiration of the old. Jackson did not favor a challenge to the bank at this time. He knew that the precipitation of the fight would inject the institution into the presidential campaign less than a year later. Even so bellicose a fighter as Benton would have postponed the struggle, but Clay was at Biddle's elbow urging action.

The bitter struggle that was to begin and continue for four years was on the demand of Clay, not Jackson. The reason is manifest. The popular orator of the Whigs went through the greater portion of his life hungering for the presidency. His nomination by the Whigs in 1832 was certain. He was seeking success at the polls. He knew that if the recharter measure was passed and vetoed by Jackson, the bank would be forced to fight and forced to pour its money into the campaign in his support. Webster, equally eager for a triumph over the man who had triumphed over the English, joined Clay in putting pressure on the bank.

Deeply disturbed and still reluctant, Biddle hurried to Washington for the historic conference with Clay and Webster. He found them still making their demands for immediate action, but he still drew back until the pressure took the form of polite blackmail. Did Biddle want to continue to have the support of Clay and Webster in the Senate? Then he must follow their advice. Again Clay gave his word that a recharter bill would pass, and, if vetoed, would be passed over Jackson's veto.

Thus, the bank fight was forced, not by the rash and prejudiced Jackson as some historians would have us believe, but by Henry Clay to serve his personal ambition. The bill was introduced. In the Senate it was referred to a committee composed of four servants of the bank and one Jacksonian. In the House the battle began with an attempt to have it referred to the Committee on Ways and Means, packed with the enemies of Jackson. That failed and the administration forces introduced numerous amendments followed by long speeches charging the bank with usury, with the issuance of bank notes by branch banks as currency, with the selling of coin, and with loaning government deposits to editors, brokers, and members of Congress.

Gravely alarmed, Biddle hurried to Washington personally to take charge,

and at the Barnard Hotel he gave elaborate dinners to members of Congress who were singularly lacking in a sense of delicacy or decency. Biddle was no ordinary money-grubber. When serving as secretary of the American legation in Paris under Monroe, he had learned the ways of diplomacy. He was a real aristocrat as well as autocrat. He was elegant and graceful in manner, suave and highly polished, schooled in literature, scintillating and amusing in conversation; and his correspondence which was to reveal much to history was as rich in charm as in indiscretions. He was clever and unscrupulous in his methods. He entertained in courtly fashion in his home in Philadelphia and in Washington, and the members of Congress who enjoyed his hospitality became the nucleus of a bank party that looked with condescension on the chief of state. Through the earnest loyalty of members of Congress who were the beneficiaries of his bounty, he was better informed on congressional gossip than the President. But, like all dictators, he was vain, and, instead of concealing his power, he flaunted it in the face of the people. Having gone to Washington, he literally lived at the Capitol, and on July 3, in the year of the presidential election, he was able to report to his directors that a bill rechartering the bank had passed Congress five years before the old charter expired.

Triumphant until then, he concentrated now on an effort to prevent a veto; almost daily he had contact with his supporters in the cabinet. But Clay was eager for a veto that would force the bank deeper into the campaign of 1832. The passage of the recharter bill had aroused the ire of Jackson. The contest now was between Emperor Nicholas, as Biddle was called, and the President of the United States. "I will prove to them," said Jackson, "that I never flinch," and his veto followed close on the passage of the measure. That veto has been criticized as an incitation to class warfare, but Jackson had not invited the contest which had been forced upon him. However, he aimed to strike sturdy blows:

It is to be regretted that the rich and powerful too often bend the acts of government to their selfish purposes. Every man is equally entitled to protection by law, but when the laws undertake to add to their natural and just advantages artificial distinctions, to grant gratuities and exclusive privileges, to make the rich richer and the powerful more potent, the humble members of society—the farmers, mechanics and laborers, who have neither the time nor means of securing like favors to themselves, have a right to complain of the injustice of their government.... Many of our rich have not been content with equal protection and equal benefits but have besought us to make them richer by acts of Congress.

The issue was then crystal clear as Jefferson had foreseen. The champions of the Hamiltonian theory that to make a government strong it must be made profitable to the powerful were in the saddle, booted and spurred. The issue that emerged was this—should the democracy of Jefferson continue or yield to a plutocracy? Should the economic rights of the common man give way to the domination of money? Should the democracy that triumphed under Jefferson end after thirty years to the Hamiltonian concept of society that Jefferson had crushed?

VII

Too few historians have seemed to realize that this was a contest on the fundamental principles of the nation. An embryo plutocracy had arisen, was in possession of leading newspapers, and had its cohorts in Congress with bank money jingling in their pockets. Even then Biddle had become the Emperor Nicholas. When he appeared in Washington, too many members of Congress flocked to Barnard's to get his orders; when a levee of the President at the White House collided with a levee of Biddle at Barnard's, too many snubbed the head of the nation to bow humbly before the head of the bank. Editors were now getting unsecured loans with the feeling that they would not be annoyed with demands for payment. At this time in the midst of the bank struggle Daniel Webster, championing the bank, wrote to Biddle, "I believe my retainer has not been renewed or refreshed as usual [note the "as usual"] and if it is wished that my relations to the bank should continue, it would be well to send me the usual retainer." This from Webster! Imagine the bank relations of lesser men.

Yes, democracy and the Jeffersonian principle of equal rights were in the twilight; the sun was warming the cohorts of plutocracy who at this time were nearer triumph than they had ever been before. But the voice of the people began to be heard over the clamor in Congress, and the bank could not muster enough votes to override the veto. This was as Clay had planned. The presidential campaign was opening, and the bank with its gold would be forced to move to his side with its moneybags. Suffice it to say that thanks to the immense popularity of Jackson and the brilliant strategy of the practical politicians of the Kitchen Cabinet, Jackson again triumphed.

But a battle, not the war, had been

won, and Jackson, who believed in the extermination of the enemy, then launched his counteroffensive after the election. His personal victory had been won, but not that of the nation. The active participation of the bank in the campaign had been notorious; the bitterness engendered had been intense; and the bank was still in position to use the government deposits in a war upon the people's government. Jackson determined to pull its fangs by the removal of the government deposits. Most of the cabinet were opposed, some through fear and some through a secret partiality for the bank. When William J. Duane, Secretary of the Treasury and a weakling partial to the bank, procrastinated, he was summarily removed, and into his place stepped a fighting man after Jackson's own heart—the brilliant Roger B. Taney, a great lawyer and jurist, a profound thinker, and a man of unimpeachable integrity who for so many years was to sit in the seat of John Marshall.

This served notice that the struggle was to the death. Biddle sent a memorial to Congress protesting against the removal of the deposits. Infuriated by Jackson's easy triumph in the election, he conceived the idea of disciplining the people. He would show his claws; he would punish the people. He began the reduction of discounts, the collection of all balances against the state banks, and most disastrous of all, the refusal of credits to business men. Factories closed because they were unable to get loans, and workers were thrown into the street. Business houses began to fail because they could not get credit. And Biddle was delighted. He wrote jubilantly after a visit to New York and Washington that only the distress of the people would force a recharter of the bank, and he gloried in the suffering.

That which Jefferson had foreseen had come to pass. A moneyed institution was serving notice of its power to penalize the people who ignored its mandates, notice that it had power to dictate legislation to serve its monopolistic ends. Biddle arranged mass meetings of his cohorts to protest the removal of the deposits, and he inspired memorials to Congress. The orators of the bank, led by Clay and supported by Webster and Calhoun, were shedding tears in bathetic speeches and wiping their eyes on the public.

It was then that Clay introduced his resolution in the Senate censuring the President of the United States who refused to do the bidding of Biddle. It was play acting at its best. The galleries had been packed with the friends of the bank, and, in a long speech trembling with compassion for the suffering people, Clay appealed to Van Buren, presiding in the chair, to plead with Jackson for the hungry and starving. But Van Buren was as consummate an actor as Clay. He sat apparently intent on treasuring in his memory all that Clay had asked him to say. When Clay sank into his seat worn by his exertion and torn by his compassion for the people, every one turned to the suave Van Buren. Calling a Senator to the chair, he descended the rostrum, every eye in the Senate on him, and, walking to the seat of Clay, he bowed in his Chesterfieldian manner and gravely requested a pinch of the orator's snuff. Taken by surprise, Clay offered his snuff box. Van Buren opened it deliberately in the dramatic silence of the chamber, and extracting a pinch of snuff applied it to his nostrils. Deliberately he closed the box, bowed again in his courtly fashion, and slowly returned to the rostrum. It was an anticlimax and the tears that Clay had shed had been dried in the sunshine of the smiles, and his appeal was lost in the tumult of the laughter.

Time was now running against the bank. Memorials against it were pouring in that had not been bought. Most disturbing of all were the memorials of state legislatures; but the climax came in the action of Governor [George] Wolf of Pennsylvania, an erstwhile supporter, who turned upon his former friends with a denunciation of the bank as responsible for the depression.

The bitter debate on the resolution of censure, supported angrily by Clay, Webster, and Calhoun, ended in its adoption, the first act of the kind in American history. Years would pass before another such insult to a President would be offered to Andrew Johnson, pilloried for the crime of battling for the constitutional rights of the South and the preservation of its civilization.

But the censure of Andrew Jackson at the behest of the bank aroused the anger of the nation. The Jacksonians never failed accurately to appraise the feeling of the people. They momentarily confined themselves to the demand that the Clay resolution of censure with the vote of each Senator should be sent to the governor of each state for transmission to his legislature. No longer could there be any doubt that the bank could create a panic and depression, could punish the people for legislation it disliked, and if permitted to continue could ultimately dictate the legislation of the future.

Meanwhile, Clay, having failed to march to the presidency over a pavement of gold laid with the money of the bank, was losing interest. He who had involved Biddle in a losing struggle was becoming

impatient with his importunities and complaints. The bank held on precariously for a time under the laws of Pennsylvania and then went down in a crash. Biddle retired to his countryseat to meditate on his blunders, and when he died, William Cullen Bryant of the New York *Evening Post* wrote that he had "died at his countryseat where he passed his last days in elegant retirement, which, if justice had been done, would have been spent in the penitentiary."

Jackson had won, but the censure rankled; and, in the closing days of the Jackson tenure in the White House, the Jacksonians, under the leadership of Benton, moved to have the censure stricken from the journal. Clay, Webster, and Calhoun made mournful speeches with Clay appearing for the occasion dressed in funereal black. In Benton's room the tables groaned under the weight of hams, turkeys, and whiskey for the refreshment of the faithful. The roll was called and the censure of one of the greatest of Americans was erased from the record in the presence of the Senators who had offered the insult.

Jackson's war on a moneyed monopoly that was presuming to dictate to the nation was his greatest service to the people. It put democracy on an even keel. It served notice that ours is a government by men and not by money. It asserted and maintained the preeminence of the people's government in the affairs of the country. It made good the Jeffersonian formula of equal rights with special privileges for none. And the arrogant plutocracy that had dared challenge the national government of all the people was buried in the grave of the national bank.

THOMAS P. ABERNETHY (1890-   ), a leading
historian of the Revolutionary and early national
periods of American history, examines in the book from
which this selection is taken, the important state
of Tennessee, believing that this type of investigation
will deepen our knowledge of the growth of American
democracy. In contrast to Frederick Jackson
Turner, he discovered the "first offspring" of the
West to be not democracy, but "arrant opportunism."
His book challenges those who see in Andrew
Jackson the ideal leader of frontier democracy.*

► | *Andrew Jackson and the New Democracy*

Deep in the consciousness of the submerged masses is ever the desire for
self-assertion, for "equality," while just
as firmly planted in the minds of the
fortunate few is the desire to control.
The developments of the Revolutionary
period had gone far toward liberating
the masses from political and economic
oppression, but it had by no means put
them in control of the government. The
period immediately following the Revolutionary era was not favorable to any
further developments along this line.
Indians and foreign powers gave trouble;
the population was engaged in the occupation of new frontiers, and strong
leadership was vital to the very life of

the new nation. The man who could
furnish this leadership was looked up to
as a public benefactor. He regarded himself in that light when he accepted public office, and if he could contrive to
make his official position contribute to
his private fortune, it was only a just
reward for his services. The small group
of leaders in any community were closely
connected, and offices were passed around
among friends and kinsmen as a matter of course.

It was the panic of 1819 which first
disturbed this peaceful order of society.
A situation similar to that which prevailed in Tennessee following the sudden collapse of the price of cotton in

* From Thomas P. Abernethy, *From Frontier to Plantation in Tennessee: A Study in
Frontier Democracy*. Memphis: Memphis State College Press, 1955. First published in 1932.
Reprinted without footnotes by permission of the author.

that year was widespread throughout the states south of New England.

The distress was probably the most acute which the nation ever suffered, for it affected not only the trading and speculating class, but a large proportion of the agricultural population as well. The courts were flooded with suits for debt, and some of them temporarily suspended proceedings on cases of this nature. In Tennessee a movement was set on foot to induce Governor [Joseph] McMinn to call a special session of the legislature in order that some form of relief might be granted the debtors. The governor, whose section of the state, East Tennessee, had come unscathed through the panic, at first failed to understand the significance of the matter, but soon he discovered which way the political winds were blowing, and the extra session was duly called.

The substantial portion of the population was generally opposed to this proceeding, but certain politicians had a different point of view. Felix Grundy had come to the state from Kentucky in 1809. His reputation as a criminal lawyer had preceded him, and he fell readily into a lucrative practice. In 1811 he had been elected to Congress in time to take a leading part with the "War Hawks" in bringing on the second conflict with England. In 1814 he retired from this post and returned to private life for a period of five years. His strength in his profession lay, not in legal learning, but in forensic persuasiveness with the jury. It was in keeping with his character that, in 1819, he should come forward as champion of the popular cause. He was the first demagogue of Tennessee and the local father of the democratic movement which, in its national phase, bears the name of Andrew Jackson.

Grundy announced himself as a candidate for a seat in the State senate on a "relief" platform, and a spirited campaign followed in the Nashville district. The popular cause triumphed, and its hero dominated the ensuing session of the legislature. The central feature of his program was the establishment of a state loan office or "bank." The capital of this institution was to be furnished by the state, its directors elected by the legislature, and its funds loaned in the different counties in proportion to the taxes paid in each. Creditors were to be induced to receive the notes of this bank by a provision that a refusal to do so would result in suspension of collection for a period of two years.

This scheme was opposed by Andrew Jackson and his neighbor and friend, Edward Ward, who argued that it made something beside gold and silver a tender in payment of debts, and hence was unconstitutional. They memorialized the legislature to this effect, but that body refused to receive the memorial on the ground that its language was disrespectful. The truth of the matter was that Jackson, in conversation, had said that any man who voted for the "stay" law was guilty of perjury, and the fate of the memorial suffered as a result of this language.

In this stand Jackson, queerly enough, found himself in alignment with East Tennessee, for that section of the state had little need of relief legislation, and its leaders were of the old school. Nevertheless, the Grundy program was passed by a strictly sectional vote, with East Tennessee on one side and Middle Tennessee on the other. The bank was established, but the directorate which the legislature cautiously selected included none who would have been apt to favor its establishment. John McNairy refused to serve as president, but John

H. Eaton accepted appointment on the board. James Jackson, a wealthy merchant of Nashville and a close friend, though no relation, to Andrew, criticized Eaton for his action, but Andrew said nothing. The assembly had responded to the popular demand but it had put the bank into the hands of conservatives. Wealthy but panic-stricken Middle Tennessee had played the demagogue again, as it had done on the land question in 1806.

The relief movement was not confined to the one state. As has been said, it affected all the country south of New England, and out of it grew the national democratic movement of the Jackson period. The masses, out of their dire need, for the first time rose up to demand relief, and they got it. Having once tasted of the heady drink of power, they were never again to resign it wholly into the hands of the politicians and the enlightened minority.

In 1821, the supreme court of Tennessee, by a vote of two out of three, decided, on the same ground taken by Jackson in 1820, that the "stay" law was unconstitutional, but the decision was held up for technical reasons. In 1822 the legislature, by an almost unanimous vote, refused to repeal the law, and in 1823 reënacted it. By this time the notes of the state bank were as good as any other available currency and the victory of Grundy was no longer significant.

Before this date momentous changes had taken place. In 1821 McMinn's third term expired, and he was not eligible for reëlection. The candidates who sought his place were Colonel Edward Ward and General William Carroll. Ward was of Virginian origin, well-educated, and a wealthy slave-owner and planter. Carroll was from Pennsylvania, a merchant and a soldier. He had opened the first nail store in Nashville, and was

owner of the first steamboat which, in 1818, reached the town. In 1811 he had taken a prominent part in the organization of a local military company, of which he was elected captain, and Jackson had helped procure arms for the command. He had served under Jackson in the Creek campaign, and had been elected to succeed his chief as major general of militia when the latter was translated to the Army of the United States. In this capacity, Carroll had commanded the Tennessee troops, constituting the left wing, at the battle of New Orleans. It was his command which withstood the heaviest shock of the British attack, and his fame was second only to that of Jackson. Shortly after this engagement he wrote to the "Hero" of the occasion and urged him to offer for the presidency of the United States, but during the next year a break occurred between the two. The reasons for this rift are obscure, but its effects were far-reaching.

Carroll had lost heavily in the panic of 1819 and was looked upon as a poor man at this time. He was touted as a simple man of the people. Ward was accused of being an aristocrat and a college-bred man who despised the poor.

The press took an active part in the campaign, the Nashville *Clarion* and Knoxville *Register* supporting Carroll, and the *Whig* and the *Gazette* of Nashville backing Ward. Jackson used all his powerful and ramifying influence in the cause of the latter, and denounced Carroll and his associates as a group of demagogues. The campaign waxed exceedingly warm, and was the most exciting that Tennessee had known since 1803 when Jackson had once before backed the wrong candidate.

It is surprising that neither of the aspirants favored the bank of 1820. They both issued statements on the subject, and both agreed that farmers could never hope to improve their situation by borrowing at 6 per cent when their agricultural operations rarely paid more than 5 per cent on the investment. Thrift and economy, they said, were the only remedies for the prevailing financial ills of the country. Yet neither candidate recommended the destruction of the bank. Ward advocated a unified state system, with a central office in Nashville and branches distributed over the state. He undoubtedly intended that this should be a regular commercial organization under private ownership, and hence entirely different from the loan office of 1820. Carroll, on the other hand, insisted on the necessity for a return to specie payments. In 1819 all the banks except the old State Bank of Knoxville, of which Hugh Lawson White was president, had suspended, and their paper now passed at a heavy discount. The notes of the new state bank were no more valuable than the others, and a return to a specie basis was of primary importance, as Carroll viewed the situation. He, as a merchant, had suffered as a result of over-trading and the consequent panic. He believed that paper money was largely responsible for all the trouble, and was ever afterward a staunch advocate of a sound specie basis for all currency. This did not involve an opposition to banks in general. It was inflation which he opposed.

Remarkably little was said of other issues during the campaign; yet it appears that Carroll let it be known he favored a revision of the state constitution which would make it possible to tax land according to its value instead of at a flat rate per hundred acres. He was definitely the people's candidate, and the returns of the election are the most direct evidence to that effect. He car-

ried every county in the state save two, East Tennessee joining West Tennessee in sweeping him into office. Jackson and the "aristocratic" party had been routed by the new leader of the democracy.

Carroll had stolen the thunder from Grundy and ushered in the second phase of the apotheosis of the people. He opposed the "stay" law and all other forms of relief legislation. He believed that banks existed for commercial purposes and should be conducted in the usual business manner. He desired a strong and independent judiciary. He believed that the lot of the masses should be ameliorated by progressive, humanitarian legislation. He insisted that a penitentiary should be established, and the criminal code revised so as to abolish the use of the pillory, the whipping post, and the branding iron.

Except for an intermission of one term, made necessary by the constitution, Carroll remained in office until 1835. During that period he succeeded in putting his reform ideas largely into practice. Not only was a penitentiary established, but an insane asylum was founded, and imprisonment for debt was abolished. Nothing interested Carroll more than the question of education, and he finally succeeded in securing substantial appropriations and the formulation of laws which sought, for the first time, to establish a system of common schools for the state. He also advocated the construction of internal improvements, and appropriations for this purpose were made during his incumbency. Under his leadership specie payments were resumed in 1826, and during the early thirties the bank of 1820 was dissolved. Meanwhile several commercial banks were chartered by the state, and a branch of the Bank of the

United States located in Nashville. The progress actually accomplished in the establishment of a school system and a system of internal improvements was discouraging; yet beginnings were made which paved the way for further progress in the succeeding period.

Perhaps the most important accomplishment of the reform governor was the calling of a constitutional convention which met in 1834 and revised the frame of government, providing for taxation of land according to value rather than at a uniform rate per hundred acres, and for the election of county officials by the people instead of by the legislature. This was the consummation of the democratic movement in the state, but it was not accomplished without arduous effort. Several proposals to call a convention had been defeated by the legislature, beginning in 1821. It was not until 1833 that the measure was finally adopted and the convention called.

The alignment in this struggle is of unusual interest. In the legislature, Middle Tennessee favored the convention, while East Tennessee opposed it. As in connection with the land question in 1806 and then again in connection with the bank of 1820, Middle Tennessee, the home of wealthy land magnates, stood for democracy against East Tennessee, the home of the small farmer. Middle Tennessee politicians in all three cases were bidding against East Tennessee politicians for the support of the people, and in every case they won. It is interesting that Andrew Jackson should have been brought up in such a school.

When the people were asked to vote for a convention, they did so by a large majority, but the alignment here was quite different from that in the legislature, and it is an unequivocal demonstration of the fact that representatives do not always speak for their constituents. There was no fencing between politicians from the two sections of the state in this case. It was altogether a question of the landed class against the poor. In the valleys of northeast Tennessee and in the Cumberland basin— the long-settled parts of the state—the vote was heavily against the convention. In the mountainous and hilly districts lying between these two areas, the vote was as heavily in its favor.

The most peculiar situation, however, existed in the old Congressional Reservation. This area included the "Western District," lying between the Tennessee and Mississippi rivers, and a broad strip extending along the southwestern border of the state. Here the lands had been opened in 1818 for the satisfaction of North Carolina warrants, and the best acreage was taken up by speculators, but no provision was made for the sale of the remainder. Thus about half the land was held out of the market and left to be occupied by squatters. This class evidently had grown to outnumber the owners, for a heavy vote in favor of the convention was cast in every county of the Reservation. There is no other way in which to account for this phenomenon, for this was one of the richest parts of the state, and certainly those who owned land here were not in favor of a change which would increase their taxes. David Crockett's district lay in this area and in Congress he devoted his attention primarily to an effort to secure lands for the squatter class.

Between 1819 and 1834 the democratic movement had gone through two phases in Tennessee. The first phase, of which [Felix] Grundy was the protagonist, stood for relief legislation and inflation of the currency in the interest of the debtor. [General William] Carroll, partly because of his personal popularity and partly because the bank of 1820 did not prove to be the financial panacea which the people had expected, arrested this development and converted the democracy to a policy of retrenchment and specie payments along with progressive social legislation. This distinguishes the movement sharply from the Populism of a later day, for the latter was clearly of the debtor-class, inflationist variety. The fact that the democracy of the thirties was of another type was due in large measure to the strong leadership of such men as Carroll, Jackson, and Thomas H. Benton. The specie policy of the Jackson period has usually been looked upon as a debtor-class program. It was in fact the policy of conservative, commercially-minded men of the period following the panic of 1819. Such men were not afraid of banks, but they were afraid of inflation.

The part played by Andrew Jackson during this period of Tennessee history is worthy of note. He was in complete accord with Carroll's economic ideas, but he gave no aid to the liberal movement which Carroll was so ably leading. Not only this, but he definitely set himself against the movement and its leader. As a result, he was discredited as a local politician at the same time that his name was being placed upon the banner of the national democratic movement, of which the local was merely one manifestation. This anomaly requires some explanation. It is therefore necessary to trace certain phases of Jackson's rise to national political fame.

It was the Battle of New Orleans, and that alone, which made Jackson a national figure. The political importance of this event was realized at once, not only by Carroll and other Tennesseans,

but also by Aaron Burr and Edward Livingston who approached the "Hero" on the subject of the presidency. But Monroe held that high office with the prospect of reëlection in 1820, and no direct move could be made until after that year. Meanwhile Jackson retained his military command.

In 1816 the General quarelled with William H. Crawford of Georgia, secretary of the treasury and heir apparent of the Virginia dynasty. In 1814 Jackson had negotiated a treaty with the Creek Indians whereby they ceded certain lands to the United States. In 1816 Crawford negotiated a treaty with the Cherokees who held conflicting claims, and the Secretary not only granted compensation for lands already ceded by the Creeks, but allowed them damages for spoilations said to have been committed by Jackson's troops when they passed through the Indian country in 1813. The Hero of New Orleans looked upon this as a malicious slur upon his military reputation, and he hated Crawford accordingly. There was also good political material in the quarrel, for Crawford was made to appear an opponent of the interests of the West, while Jackson was the avowed champion of the cause of the frontier.

His reputation as an expansionist was increased two years later when he was sent to the Florida border to punish the Seminole Indians for certain raids which they had made across the line. On this occasion he wrote to President Monroe stating if it should be signified to him through John Rhea, a congressman from East Tennessee and an old friend to the General, that it was desirable to take possession of the Floridas, he would do it without further authorization. Rhea wrote, giving Jackson to understand that Monroe approved the plan. Pensacola was taken and Jackson was attacked in the Cabinet and the Senate. He went to Washington to face his enemies, but he burned the Rhea letter at the request of its author. Monroe supported Jackson who had supported him in 1808, but did not admit that he had authorized the attack on Pensacola. The burning of the Rhea letter, which might have cleared up the situation considerably, was apparently a magnanimous act on the part of Jackson in order to save his friend from the embarrassment of having Monroe disavow his right to speak for him.

In 1821 Jackson resigned from the army and was appointed governor of Florida by Monroe. The General accepted the Commission as a public vindication by the President of his conduct in the Seminole affair. But Florida was always unkind to Jackson, and he gave up his place before the year was over, having gone through several trying experiences which added to his reputation for overbearing conduct. He now returned to the Hermitage, ostensibly to retire to "the pleasures of domestic felicity," but actually to run for the presidency.

At about this time there was formed in Nashville a little group of three men who took upon themselves the responsibility for the future political career of the Hero of New Orleans. Of these, William B. Lewis is perhaps the best known. He had come to Nashville at an early date, and it appears that he was for some years proprietor of the Nashville Inn. He had married a daughter of William Terrell Lewis, who was not a kinsman. This young woman, upon her father's death, had become the ward of General Jackson. It was through this marriage that William B. Lewis came into possession of the homestead of his wife's father, located near the Hermitage. Here an intimate friendship had grown up between Jackson and Lewis long before the General became famous at New Orleans.

John H. Eaton, whose home was at Franklin near Nashville, and who later married the notorious Peggy O'Neill, had married for his first wife another daughter of William Terrell Lewis. It was doubtless through this connection that he became associated with Jackson. As early as 1813, he was acquainted with certain of the General's friends. In 1816 he undertook to write a life of "Old Hickory" and at that time was unknown to fame. In 1818 he was appointed to the United States Senate, and in 1819 defended Jackson against his detractors in that body, who were being led on by John Williams, the senator from East Tennessee. These facts would make it appear that Jackson had taken a personal interest in Eaton and had used his influence to bring him into public notice. Eaton stood ready to repay the debt, and now became the second member of the Nashville trio. His position in the Senate made him an especially valuable member.

The third member of the group was John Overton, with whom Jackson had boarded at the widow Donelson's when he first came to Tennessee, with whom he had practiced law in the frontier days, and with whom he had been closely associated in many ways during all the intervening years. Eaton and Lewis were followers of the General. Overton was his backer, his friend, and his adviser. Eaton and Lewis went to Washington and received office at Jackson's hand. Overton stayed in Nashville and received nothing, but he remained a staunch friend until the day of his death, and burned his political correspondence in order that curious eyes might not pry into the details of the campaign. He was one of the richest men in Tennessee:

he had been a member of the state supreme court, and had many business interests. He was the most distinguished member of the group, but is the least known because he remained in the background, demanding no reward for his services.

There was nothing in the composition of this coterie or in the record of Jackson himself to connect his candidacy with the democratic movement which was in full tide in Tennessee under the leadership of Carroll. Eaton, Lewis, and Overton were all conservative men of the old school, who were interested in government for what they could get out of it. Not one of them could be considered a man of the people. They did not come out openly and oppose the new movement as did Jackson, because they were more cautious, but the opinion of men of their type was well expressed by one Thomas Emmerson, a friend to Overton, and at one time a colleague of his on the state supreme court. In letters addressed to his friend, he denounced manhood suffrage and the idea that an office-holder should be looked upon as a servant of the people and amenable to instruction from his constituents. He did not intend to seek office, he said, nor to accept a place under the assumption that the people were doing him a favor to give it to him. He considered the favor was the other way round, and he was true to his convictions. There is no better illustration of the spirit of the old school as it passed from the scene. Jackson and his allies were also of the old school, but they had no very strong convictions and were willing to make friends with the times. It is not the greatest men who go to the top in politics.

In spite of the conservatism of Jackson and his friends and their coldness toward

the liberal movement in Tennessee, the victorious liberals did not hesitate to support the candidacy of the "Hero" for the presidency. His only important local opposition consisted of a few personal enemies, while East Tennessee under the leadership of Hugh Lawson White, and West Tennessee under the leadership of the Nashville trio, united for the first time on an important issue. Strangely enough, it was Felix Grundy, originally favorable to Henry Clay and never liked by Jackson, who took upon himself the leadership of the Jackson cause in the legislature. Grundy was astute enough to see that since state pride over the prospect of having a son in the White House was so great as to cause all sections to drop their differences and unite in the interest of Jackson's candidacy, he could do no better by his own career than to fall into line.

In 1823 it became necessary for John Williams, the Tennessee senator who had attacked Jackson on the Seminole issue in 1818, to present himself before the legislature for reëlection. It would not look well for the General's presidential candidacy abroad for his avowed enemy to remain in office in his own state. In order therefore that he should be defeated, it became necessary for Jackson himself, at the last minute, to announce himself as an opposition candidate. He won the contest and returned to the body from which he had resigned in 1798. Here he voted consistently in favor of internal improvements and the protective tariff, thus taking a definite stand on the most important issues of the day. After having served for little more than a year, he retired in favor of Hugh Lawson White.

It is clear that in the campaign of 1824 Jackson stood before the country as a nationalist, favoring vigorous exercise of the powers of the Federal government. This would appear to have been inconsistent with his "Tertium Quid"* connections of 1808 and with his general profession of strict Jeffersonian principles. As late as 1822 he wrote to Monroe to congratulate him upon the veto of the Cumberland road bill. Then, after having voted for improvements in 1824, he stated in 1826 that he believed the Federal government to have the right to construct them only with the consent of the state within which the work was to be done. During the next year his Tennessee following in the legislature opposed the policy. Thus he had apparently completed the circle and swung back to his first opinion.

On the question of the tariff he was decidedly at odds with his own constituents. Tennessee, though never a cotton state on a large scale, was controlled chiefly by cotton planters, to which class Jackson himself belonged. Like the cotton states, she never really believed in a protective tariff. In 1824 Jackson defended protection on the ground that it was necessary to build up manufactures for military reasons, and for the creation of a home market for surplus agricultural products. It is possible that his point of view as a military man was responsible for his stand, and it is also possible that his desire for the presidency influenced his opinion. It was hardly a strict-constructionist stand.

In the campaign of 1824 Jackson considered William H. Crawford, of Georgia, his most dangerous opponent

* The name applied to a group of politicians in Virginia led by John Randolph of Roanoke, who, in the election of 1808, sought to nominate Monroe as the Republican candidate for President. After they failed to obtain either the cooperation of Monroe or the necessary alliance with the New England Federalists, the movement collapsed—Ed.

Crawford had attacked him in the Cabinet during the Seminole controversy of 1818, and now, as the anointed of the Virginia dynasty and the champion of state rights, was running against him for the presidency. John C. Calhoun was also a member of the Cabinet in 1818. Jackson had understood that the Carolinian supported him during the disturbance of that year, and now Calhoun joined forces with Jackson and accepted the second place on his ticket.

Before 1828 came around to bring about the second Jackson campaign, many important changes had taken place. One of the most interesting of these was that Crawford had withdrawn from the race, and only John Quincy Adams stood against "Old Hickory." In 1824 Crawford had been supported by Martin Van Buren of New York. With Crawford's withdrawal, Van Buren was left free to make a new alliance, and this time he threw his support to Jackson. When the General went to New Orleans to celebrate, on January 8, 1828, the victory which had been won thirteen years previously on the plains of Chalmette, the Republican organization of New York sent as its representative on that auspicious occasion Colonel James A. Hamilton. It was under these circumstances Hamilton suggested to Lewis and Jackson that Crawford might be brought into the camp. Certain moves to this end had been made the previous year, and why not? Van Buren had supported Crawford in 1824; why should Crawford not support Van Buren in 1828? Yet this probably would involve a break with Calhoun. Jackson had been informed on good authority in 1824 that Calhoun had not been his friend in 1818 as he had supposed and as Calhoun had allowed him to believe. But the General would not credit this report at the time, nor did he admit suspicion of his run-ning-mate in 1828.

These circumstances, however, would make it appear that the clever little "Red Fox" of New York had his plans well laid. It would not be difficult for him to induce Crawford to expose Calhoun's unfavorable attitude toward Jackson in the Cabinet when that body was investi-gating the Seminole affair. Such an exposé would pave the way for Van Buren to supplant the South Carolinian in the estimation of General Jackson. All this came about in due season. Van Buren's plans had a way of turning out as he intended they should. The affair of Peggy Eaton was merely a windfall which tumbled into his lap.

Jackson, as president, took a stand against internal improvements. New York had dug the Erie Canal and did not care to have the Federal government assist Pennsylvania to construct a com-peting system. Van Buren, in league with the state rights school of Virginia, admitted his influence in this connection.

Jackson's war on the Bank of the United States is usually considered to have been in line with his earlier views, but the evidence to this effect is al-together *post hoc.* He himself said that he began to distrust the Bank when in 1825 he read of the South Sea Bubble explosion. He did not begin to manifest this hostility before 1827, and it seems fairly clear that his opposition became active only when he realized that the influence of some of the branches of the Bank were being used against his election. It was characteristic of him to form his opinions on such a basis. Van Buren denied his influence in this matter, but New York had her safety fund system, and the Bank was located at Philadelphia. Henry Clay believed that the New Yorker, in collaboration

with Virginia politicians, was responsible for the charge. William B. Lewis, repre-senting Tennessee interests, was opposed to a break with the Bank.

Thus the nationalist senator of 1823 became the state rights president of 1829. Van Buren gave to Democracy the plat-form under which it became the champion of strict construction and was finally transformed from the party of the West to that of the cotton-growing South and the slaveocracy. Jackson's nullification proclamation was hardly in line with state rights doctrines, what-ever one may have thought of the right of nullification. Jackson was not a theorist. He was a man of action and an opportunist. He always maintained that he was a believer in state rights, but is usually classified as a nationalist. It is impossible, in fact, to classify him as belonging strictly to either school of thought, for he bestraddled them.

Not only was Jackson not a consistent politician, he was not even a real leader of democracy. He had no part whatever in the promotion of the liberal move-ment which was progressing in his own state under the leadership of William Carroll. His advisers and friends were conservative men of the old school who rather opposed than assisted the new movement. The democracy of America called him to be its leader because he was a westerner with a colorful person-ality and a transcendent military reputa-tion. He was a self-made man, generous and dynamic, but he was not a progres-sive politician. Brought up in the old school of William Blount,* he always

* William Blount was a large-scale spec-ulator, territorial governor, and United States Senator. He was for many years the dominant political power in Tennessee. As Jackson's patron and political benefactor, he was responsible for the rapid rise of the young lawyer in state politics—Ed.

believed in making the public serve the ends of the politician. Democracy was good talk with which to win the favor of the people and thereby accomplish ulterior objectives. Jackson never really championed the cause of the people; he only invited them to champion his. He was not consciously hypocritical in this. It was merely the usual way of doing business in those primitive and ingenuous times. An illustration will probably clarify the point In 1798 Jackson condemned the Federalists for using office for partisan purposes. In 1829 he wrote to a friend that he had many applications for office and "so far as real charitable objects presented themselves, I have yielded my might to their relief." He intended, he said, to turn the spies out of the camp. Turning the spies out may have been all right, but using office for charitable purposes was a rather private way of dealing with the public business.

CHARLES M. WILTSE (1907-   ), in his three-volume biography of Calhoun, wrote one of the more complete and impressive analyses of the Jackson era. Like Abernethy, he is a meticulous and scholarly historian whose work is both thorough and profound. In his pages Calhoun becomes the far-seeing statesman, strong in character and steadfast in principle. Jackson assumes the role of a popular but indiscreet and quick tempered authoritarian, while his political lieutenants are not infrequently placemen more interested in power and spoil than in maintaining constitutional government or in consistency to announced policies.*

King Andrew

1

When Congress assembled on December 3, 1832, the Senate was again under the necessity of electing a President pro tempore. [Littleton W.] Tazewell [senator from Virginia] had resigned his seat late in October, on the ground that as part of a hopeless minority he could accomplish nothing for his state. Calhoun was still in South Carolina; but it was already known in Washington, and pretty generally over the country, that he was to replace [Robert Y.] Hayne as Senator and so would not return to the chair of the Senate. The President pro tempore, therefore, would be the permanent presiding officer for the remainder of the Congress; and whoever held that post would be automatically barred from taking more than a nominal part in the stormy debates over the tariff and nullification that were anticipated. It was for that reason that George Poindexter [of Mississippi], who had been Tazewell's closest competitor for the honor at the previous session, withdrew his own name before the balloting started.

The voting quickly concentrated on Hugh Lawson White of Tennessee and John Tyler of Virginia, with Tyler throwing his own strength to White on the fifth ballot. The arrangement meant that the President and the acting Vice President would be from the same state,

* From Charles M. Wiltse, *John C. Calhoun, Nullifier, 1829-1839.* Indianapolis: The Bobbs-Merrill Co., 1949. Reprinted without footnotes by permission of the author.

but Tyler was willing to trust that situation to White's sense of propriety. So apparently were the other Senators. On the whole, the choice was excellent. White was the candidate of the administration but he was in every way acceptable, both to the National Republicans and to the Nullifiers. Although a close friend of Jackson's, the Tennessee Senator had steadfastly refused to accept office at the hands of the President. Lean, dour, puritanical, he was a man who would follow his conscience wherever it led him. The decisions of the chair would be inflexible but impartial, and the small band of State Rights Democrats would have their full strength available on the floor.

The brief sitting on December 4 was devoted to the reading of the President's message. Calhoun, Clay, and Webster, the giants who were to dominate the proceedings of the next three months, were not yet in Washington; and it looked for a time as though they would have little to do when they came, so mild, moderate, and conciliatory was the message. After the usual summary of foreign relations, the President congratulated the country and the Congress on the payment of the public debt. It was, he declared, an occasion that called for prompt reduction of the revenue to the needs of the government. He expressed the hope that the reduction could be so accomplished as to "remove those burthens which shall be found to fall unequally" on any of the great interests of the nation; and he recommended that "the whole scheme of duties be reduced to the revenue standard as soon as a just regard to the faith of the government and the preservation of the large capital invested in establishments of domestic industry will permit." Less than six months earlier he had ac-

cepted the tariff of 1832 as the permanent policy of the country. He now denied that the protective system had ever been intended as more than temporary and incidental, and with ironic understatement noted that it tended "to beget in the minds of a large portion of our countrymen a spirit of discontent and jealousy dangerous to the stability of the union."

Jackson ended his passage on the tariff with a reference to the obstruction of the revenue collections "in one quarter" of the country and expressed the hope that prudence, patriotism, and good sense would solve the difficulty. He left the impression that, should it become impossible to execute the existing law at any point, he would lay the matter before Congress.

Having gone so far, the President went farther still and made his own the rest of Calhoun's original platform. He recommended that the public lands ought to be sold for no more than enough to cover the expense of administering the land system, and suggested that the disposal of the soil ought to be surrendered to the states. The only other important reference in the message was one questioning the safety of the public money on deposit in the Bank of the United States and its branches.

The tone and substance of the message could not have been wholly unexpected. Led by the *Globe,* the administration press had been emphasizing tariff reduction for ten days or more; and the press reflected fairly accurately the popular wish, so far as it could be learned. Particularly in New York there was a strong desire to adjust the duties to pacify the South, with Van Buren's partisans trying to outdo Clay's. Van Buren himself was understood to have declared a general amnesty for all his old foes, excepting only Calhoun. Now that the election was safely won and no votes could be lost in Pennsylvania, the Vice President-elect was out to get for himself any credit there might be for securing a modification of the protective system. On the day the message was read, the *Globe* called for reduction of the tariff to "the standard of a safe and prudent, moderate, but adequate revenue. —Not because that measure is demanded by menaces; but because it is just in itself, and is due to the feelings of an important section of the country. . . ." Three days later [Francis P.] Blair [editor of the *Globe*] was even arguing that the election was a clear victory for tariff reduction and that Calhoun had forced through the Ordinance of Nullification solely to get credit for the adjustment. The tariff, in other words, was to be reduced, and each side hoped to make political capital of it.

The reaction to Jackson's tariff proposals was generally favorable. The South was pleased and relieved. The high-tariff men, to be sure, were inclined to feel that their interests had been surrendered "to the nullifiers of the South and the land-robbers of the West"; and Southern spokesmen felt that a vast deal of suffering and ill feeling might have been spared had Jackson shown half the zeal for tariff reform in 1829 that he now showed three years later. Even Duff Green, who no longer denied that his paper was the organ of the Nullifiers, praised the message, complaining only that Jackson had not been explicit on state interposition.

He did not have long to wait for his answer. On December 10 the President issued a Proclamation against the Nullifiers. Relief turned to dismay, and pleasure to hot indignation. In terse and commanding prose the Proclamation declared that the National Government was sovereign and indivisible, that no state could refuse to obey the law, that no state could leave the Union. It closed with a direct appeal to the people of South Carolina, who were told they had been led by deluded or designing leaders to the brink of treason; and it left no doubt that the whole force of the United States would be used if need be to collect the duties in the rebellious state. The argument of the Proclamation was that of Webster in the second reply to Hayne, and of John Marshall in half a dozen leading decisions of the Supreme Court. It was written, however, in the language of the layman, and it compressed all that the great champions of nationalism had said into a fraction of the space they took to say it.

Yet able and powerful as it was, it went too far for its purpose and its time. Its reasoning, though cogent and compelling, destroyed not nullification alone, but the whole theory of State Rights from which the doctrine of interposition had been derived. When it proclaimed the government to be no federation but a consolidated whole with sovereign power vested in the majority, it went far beyond the purposes of the founding fathers, and ran directly counter to widely accepted beliefs of the time. The net effect, therefore, was not to isolate the leaders in South Carolina but to arouse all those who feared concentrated power, by whomsoever exercised. New party lines were drawn, and the Nullifiers found support where none had been expected.

Jackson himself probably failed to grasp the finer points of political theory involved, but his understanding of the reactions of the common man was, as usual, incomparable. As Benton put it, the "mass of the people think the Union is attacked, and that the Proclamation is to save it, and that brief view is decisive with them." Yet farseeing men the country over realized that to establish the political philosophy of the Proclamation meant in the end the abolition of slavery and probably the destruction of the Union. In four short years Jackson had led his party from bitter opposition to the "consolidating" tendencies of John Quincy Adams to a form of authoritarianism that outdid even the Alien and Sedition Acts of Adams' father. The individualistic democracy of the frontier lost ground to the cult of power so dear to wealth and property. The South, with its common interest and its common fear, began to coalesce, and sectional cleavage began to assume an ideological content. If any single date can be fixed as that on which a given event was predetermined, the Civil War became inevitable on December 10, 1832.

(Jackson's proclamation on Nullification)

2

The various steps taken by the administration after the passage of the Ordinance of Nullification in South Carolina fit together into a well worked out pattern. The Proclamation was a warning that the state would be crushed if she persisted in opposing the law, but the annual message had contained an explicit promise that the law would be changed. Jackson informed his aides that he meant to have the leading Nullifiers "arrested and arraigned for treason," and indicated that military force would be used if needed. Yet a member of the Cabinet, acting unofficially and incognito but on the President's orders, pointed out the danger of victory for either side and asked Virginia to act as mediator. The Cabinet member was Lewis Cass, the Secretary of War, and his overtures were

made through Thomas Ritchie [editor] of the Richmond *Enquirer.*

If Cass was indeed following privately given orders from the President, then the Proclamation was largely bluff; and the masterly caution of the Secretary's military preparations seem to bear this out. He sent Major General Winfield Scott, the second ranking officer in the Army, to take command in South Carolina, with orders to stay out of trouble at almost any cost. Again and again Cass emphasized to Scott the "anxiety of the President to avoid, if possible, a resort to force." He was, of course, to repel attack, but he was to lean over backward to avoid giving any possible provocation for attack; and nowhere in Scott's orders was there ever a word about arresting anybody, for treason or anything else.

The *Globe,* meanwhile, with the rest of the administration press tagging in its wake, hammered endlessly on the theme that nullification was treason and Calhoun the archtraitor, who had failed to win the Presidency of the whole Union and so sought now to break it that he might rule at least a part. The real purpose of the Nullifiers and the actual state of affairs in South Carolina were carefully concealed, while it was made to appear that Jackson had all along intended to reform the tariff and relieve the people of the South from their unjustly heavy burden of taxation.

The strategy, in short, was to yield the point but to destroy Calhoun. His danger was personal, physical, and very real, and no one knew it better than he did.

3

More than a month was allowed to pass before Jackson followed up his Proclamation—a month in which the reaction of all sections and classes could be ascertained and a majority in Congress could be lined up. The Proclamation had split the Jackson ranks wide open, but it had split the opposition also. Ritchie praised the Proclamation as well as the annual message; Benton "could not concur" in some of its doctrines, but was willing to accept it because he expected Jackson to destroy the Bank; Sam Houston, in Texas, read the document "with much pride and inexpressible satisfaction." [John] Floyd [governor of Virginia] saw civil war as now inevitable; to the Nullifiers it was "the black Cockade Federalism of '98 revived fearfully invigorated by its long sleep, and ... destined to bring about another reign of terror." [Churchill C.] Cambreleng [Congressman from New York] denounced it, and Van Buren himself tried to get Jackson to tone down some of the doctrines he had expressed.

The National Republicans were similarly divided. Webster placed himself under the administration banner, but Clay found many things in the Proclamation that he could not stomach. Philip Hone, who spoke for the mercantile class in New York, meant the highest praise when he called it "just such a paper as Alexander Hamilton would have written and Thomas Jefferson condemned." One New England disciple of Hamilton thought the South would be driven from the Union; but another thought the Proclamation a meaningless gesture to cover up the discomfiture of the administration. Hezekiah Niles, the high priest of the American System, called Hayne's official answer "a very ably written and strong paper"; and Judge [Joseph] Story [of the Supreme Court], whose famous *Commentaries* were almost ready for the press, thought that Jackson expressed "the true principles of the Constitution." For the abolitionists,

Garrison pronounced the Proclamation "an exceedingly powerful and eloquent exposition of the Constitution and Laws."

Such was the state of feeling when news reached Washington that Calhoun was on his way to the Capital. It was almost universally believed that Jackson would have the South Carolinian arrested as soon as he arrived and would make short work of his trial for treason. And all too many, thanks to the misrepresentations of the *Globe* and its satellites and the unguarded tongue of the President, believed him guilty and were only too willing to see him hanged.

Calhoun did not actually leave South Carolina until two weeks after his election to the Senate, although Congress was already in session. The reason for the delay, however, was not any fear of Andrew Jackson but the serious illness of Mrs. Calhoun, brought on perhaps by the nervous strain of the past weeks. It was December 22 before Floride's health was so far restored as to permit her husband to leave. He stayed briefly in Columbia to confer with Hayne, and reached Raleigh, North Carolina, on December 30. From Raleigh he went to Richmond, and arrived in Washington on January 3. Everywhere he was an object of curiosity, often of apprehension and disdain. Crowds gathered to look upon him as years before they had looked at Aaron Burr. So thoroughly had the *Globe* done its work that Calhoun was regarded as a man whose mad ambition would stop at nothing; and prejudice against him, even in the South, was bitter. He was aware of Jackson's threats against his person and fully conscious of the hostility he met along the way, but he remained outwardly calm and undaunted. Tall, erect, with flashing eyes and rugged features crowned by a shock of dark wiry hair, he was a commanding —even a noble—figure as he faced hostile mobs and asked no quarter. His passionate sincerity was so obvious that even lifelong foes, after seeing him, accorded him grudging admiration.

In Raleigh he talked for hours to shifting crowds in the great hall of the hotel. He tried to explain what nullification meant and assured his audience that there would be no breach of the peace in South Carolina unless citizens of the state were attacked by Federal troops. In Richmond he attended, as guest of Governor Floyd, a session of the Virginia legislature, which was debating a report of its special committee on Federal relations. News of his progress preceded him to Washington, but no hostile demonstration greeted his arrival. In that city where he had lived so long and was so intimately known, it was beyond the power even of Andrew Jackson or Francis Preston Blair to paint him in the image of a Catiline. "However he may now err," wrote Margaret Bayard Smith, who was both an old friend and an old political foe, "he is one of the noblest and most generous spirits I have ever met with. I am certain *he* is deceived himself, and believes he is now fulfilling the duty of a *true patriot*."

Right or wrong, deceived or a little more clearheaded than his fellows, Calhoun's courage was superb. Alone, unfaltering, with head erect and steady eyes, he walked slowly and deliberately into the Senate chamber at noon on Friday, January 4, 1833, and presented his credentials as Senator from South Carolina. For almost eight years he had sat in that same chamber as presiding officer. A dozen of the forty-eight men who then constituted the Senate of the United States had served with him in Congress during the trying years of the War of

1812, and still others had been his friends and partisans in bygone Presidential campaigns. A few stepped up and shook his hand, but most of them held back. The galleries were crowded, but ominously still, as Calhoun stood before the President pro tempore, raised his right hand, and in a solemn, clearly audible voice took the oath to uphold and defend the Constitution of the United States. Others congratulated him then, and the ice was broken.

The question of tariff reduction was already before both houses of Congress, with every indication of administration support. It would not be the administration, however, nor Martin Van Buren, who would get the credit for modifying the long-contested protective policy. It would be John C. Calhoun, and the South thereafter would be his. In the House a sweeping tariff-reduction bill hastily prepared by the Committee on Ways and Means, and called the Verplanck bill after the committee's chairman, reached the floor on January 8. The Verplanck bill was understood to be a Van Buren measure and to have the full support of the administration. Even to Calhoun the road to peace looked relatively clear, until Stephen D. Miller touched off another explosion by presenting to the Senate on January 11 resolutions of the South Carolina legislature denouncing Jackson's Proclamation. The following evening Silas Wright of New York, who had just arrived in Washington to take the seat in the Senate vacated by Marcy's election as Governor, called on the President. Because the new Senator was a confidential friend of Van Buren's, Jackson talked freely and made no secret of his intention of disciplining Calhoun, [James] Hamilton, [Jr.]* and

*Hayne's immediate predecessor as governor of South Carolina—Ed.

Hayne. He expected to save the rest of the South by reducing the tariff, but South Carolina he apparently preferred to punish. He seemed to feel, in fact, that anyone who sought to save Calhoun from the noose was trying to disgrace both the country and Andrew Jackson.

Calhoun did not know, of course, that Jackson had so recently repeated his threats when he introduced on January 14 a resolution calling on the Executive to lay before the Senate copies of the Proclamation, the counterproclamation of Governor Hayne, the South Carolina Ordinance, and other documents in the nullification controversy. It would have made no difference, however, had he known that the hangman awaited him outside the door of the Senate chamber. His was the same stubborn Scotch-Irish stock as Jackson's own, and he was no more likely to yield a conviction than was the President. In the normal order of procedure, Calhoun's resolution would have been called up for argument the following day. He acquiesced, however, when Felix Grundy asked him to let the matter rest. According to the Tennessee Senator, the documents requested were already on the way, together with a message from the President, and were expected on the seventeenth.

Anticipating no important business on the intervening day, Calhoun came late to the Senate, only to find that the documents had already arrived and the President's message was being read. And what a message it was! Calhoun sat rigidly in his seat, his eyes blazing with mounting fury as he listened. The doctrines of the Proclamation were repeated, and Jackson was asking bluntly for power to make them good. He wanted no less than authority to alter or abolish ports of entry where duties could not be collected, power to remove causes from state to Federal courts at his discretion, and authority to employ military force to execute the laws. The language of the message was carefully guarded, not asking outright for the powers in question, but suggesting the revival of long-dead statutes under which in times of Federalist dominance they had existed. There was nothing guarded, however, in the direct reference to South Carolina. The state was declared to be "in the attitude of hostile preparation" and ready for "military violence," and the President announced his intention to regard "aggression ... as committed when it is officially authorized, and the means of enforcing it fully provided."

When the reading was over, Grundy moved reference to the Committee on the Judiciary, but Calhoun was on his feet as soon as the motion had been made. For almost sixteen years he had not taken part in legislative debates, and he was to speak now without preparation because he had not expected the question to arise for another day. He was, moreover, out of order, because he meant to speak not to Grundy's motion but on the message itself. This he conceded at the outset, throwing himself on the indulgence of the Senate. No one objected, and for perhaps half an hour he held the floor.

Rarely if ever has a maiden speech in the Senate or in any other legislative body been made under more trying circumstances, or impressed itself more forcefully upon those who heard it. Calhoun's usually mobile features were expressionless as chiseled granite, his body rigid and tense as that of an animal at bay. Only his lips moved, but from them poured a torrent of words with incredible rapidity: words of biting scorn and passionate rejection. His expressive eyes, now black as coals, now flaming with the intensity of his excitement, darted restlessly about the room. The very bonds of language were powerless to chain his feelings. He was defiant, impassioned, and superb.

He changed no opinions as to the right or wrong of South Carolina's action, but he won for himself the respect if not the admiration of his foes. Original Jackson partisans who would have hanged him ten days before rushed up to grasp his hand, and men in the galleries wept unashamedly. Jackson was told that Calhoun's speech had failed, and promised again to "strike at the head" as soon as the first overt act should be committed. Webster felt a little sorry for a man he regarded as broken, and resolved to avoid any personal unkindness. But John Tyler, scion of the old Virginia school and as independent as any man alive, was jubilant. "Calhoun met the thing," he wrote gleefully to Floyd, "in a style which I have never heard surpassed—his manner was different from anything I ever heard from him before—warm—impassioned—burning—He repelled with indignation the charge of his State desiring a dissolution. ... Rely upon it that he is more than a match for all opponents." Even Churchill C. Cambreleng, although his sympathies certainly lay elsewhere, was inclined to agree with Tyler's conclusion.

So were the Senate, the Congress, and the country itself divided over the character and motives of one man. There was no middle ground, no compromise, no no-man's land. He attracted, or he repelled; he convinced, or he antagonized; he was loved, or he was hated. He was the pure and unsullied patriot, ready to sacrifice position, honors, life itself for the liberties of his country; or he was the very image of Lucifer—the archangel fallen, damned forever to the bottomless pit by his own overmastering ambition. Toward Calhoun indifference was impossible.

Calhoun himself said nothing about his speech, but he credited the President's message with advancing his own cause. For the message had completed the work the Proclamation had begun, and had so aroused the Southern members of both houses that a united South was certain within six months if the tariff was not modified. When that happened, the "doctrines of 98" would be successful again, and would "again save the Republick." Calhoun had been unable to trace the still persistent rumor that his own arrest had been ordered, but he did not doubt that Jackson, like Macbeth, saw in his dreams "the image of a Crown." With his every exercise of executive indiscretion, Jackson forced his opponents closer together. Differences of opinion on tariff, bank, or public lands were less important than agreement on the preservation of constitutional government. Clay merely echoed Calhoun when he wrote that nothing was any longer certain save that "the will of Andrew Jackson is to govern."

Within a week Calhoun was on the offensive, carrying the fight to the administration. On January 21 the Judiciary Committee reported a bill authorizing the use of force to collect the revenues, and the next day William Wilkins of Pennsylvania, the committee chairman, sought to fix a time for debate. Wilkins proposed a lapse of only two days; Miller sought to postpone the whole question until the tariff had been acted on. After some discussion, Monday, January 28, was agreed to, but immediately Calhoun was on his feet. The Force Bill rested on the same constitutional theory as the message and the Proclamation. The

South Carolina Senator offered a set of three resolutions, carefully designed to challenge that constitutional theory. The Force Bill, it had just been agreed, would not be debated for another week, but Calhoun might call up his resolutions the next day. If he could center the discussion on them rather than on the bill, he would have the right to the final speech. If, moreover, he could get his resolutions adopted, the Force Bill would collapse without a hearing because it would then be patently unconstitutional. He had not presided over the Senate for eight years without learning how to take every advantage offered by its rules.

In introducing his resolutions, Calhoun spoke briefly—again for no more than half an hour. The emotional excitement of his earlier effort was gone. He was terse, concise, and icily calm. There was not a superfluous word or thought, and no possibility of doubt in his challenge. "But two modes of political existence can long endure in our country; the one that formed, by the framers of our admirable constitution, a federal system, uniting free and independent States in a bond of union for mutual advantages, and to be preserved by the concurrent consent of the parts; or a government of the sword. The choice is before us." The administration forces, already divided and ill at ease over Jackson's highhanded methods, were threatened with a rout at the hands of this one man alone. For they had not only to win the support of both houses of Congress, they had to keep public opinion on their side as well; and Calhoun's courageous, singlehanded battle no less than his clear, incisive words was making it harder day by day to justify forcible intervention in South Carolina. The power to coerce one state was the power to coerce them all; and there was

hardly a state in the Union that had not been at one time or another in opposition to the general government.

4

In South Carolina the belligerent attitude of the administration served only to make the party cleavage sharper and the danger more real. Jackson's Proclamation set the state legislature aflame. Defiant resolutions were immediately passed, and the Governor was instructed to issue his unyielding counterproclamation and to mobilize the militia. The timorous resigned themselves to bloodshed and financial ruin. Hayne's proclamation came on December 20 and the following day he named his military aides, including James H. Hammond and Francis W. Pickens. Detailed instructions for mobilization and arming of the state troops were issued the day after Christmas. Yet even as he gave orders for raising a South Carolina army, Hayne continued to insist that he and his party wanted neither disunion nor civil war. "We have been compelled to nullify," he wrote privately to a New York correspondent, "after 10 years of patient endurance & remonstrance, as the only means left to cause our complaints to be attended to."

As there had been from the start, there were conservatives and radicals within the Nullification party—conservatives like Hayne, who would call out the militia but would take every precaution to avoid a clash and accept any reasonable compromise on the tariff as a victory; and radicals like [Robert Barnwell] Rhett who wanted to strike the first blow by seizing the government arsenals. Fortunately the conservatives were in command; and when the Virginia legislature sent Benjamin Watkins Leigh to Columbia as an official emissary from that state with instructions to urge postponement, they turned it to account. They wanted Virginia, should they yield to her mediation, to guarantee her support if the tariff was not modified; but they saw that Leigh's mission could be used to play for time.

So it fell out that shortly after Leigh's arrival in South Carolina the effective date of the Ordinance was deferred until the fourth of March. The postponement was the work of a State Rights party meeting in Charleston on January 21 and had no semblance of legality about it. The action met, however, with popular approval. It was the date Calhoun and Hayne had sought from the convention in the first place, and so the Governor discreetly took the party vote as binding without seeking to reassemble the convention to vote on it. Almost immediately thereafter news arrived that the Force Bill had been reported from committe, and excitement flared again. Sober South Carolinians saw no alternative but to withdraw from the Union if the Force Bill passed and tariff reduction did not. The demand for arms exceeded *"five times over* the number in possession of the State," and two emissaries were sent north to purchase more.

The Unionists formed military companies of their own, armed from the Federal arsenals with weapons issued by General Scott. Now and again clashes between Unionists and Nullifiers seemed imminent, but always they were avoided by the extraordinary caution and self-restraint of the latter. There was, however, a subtle change in the atmosphere. Where [Joel R.] Poinsett had earlier assured Jackson that South Carolina could put her own house in order, with the aid of government arms, he conceded by mid-January that the revenue laws could not be enforced except at the point of Federal bayonets. His own followers,

most of them, would not move against their fellows. As the Nullifiers gained the upper hand, Poinsett cast caution to the winds and begged the President to strike the first blow. While Calhoun's stature grew with each move he made in the Senate and with every threat Jackson hurled against him, Poinsett writhed and pleaded with the President not to make a martyr of his enemy.

When Jackson later showed genuine relief at the prospect that the Ordinance of Nullification would be repealed, Poinsett went so far as to urge no tariff reduction until the following session of Congress, lest the Nullifiers be the ones to reap the profit from it. If Jackson's perceptions had been as quick as his temper, it would have been clear to him from the start of his correspondence with Poinsett that the South Carolina Unionist leaders were far more eager for a clash of arms than the Nullifiers. It is not those in power, but those who have been rejected at the polls, who seek external aid for an appeal to the sword.

The crisis was over for all practical purposes by early February, and the state settled back to await the turn of events in Washington. The conservative wing of the State Rights and Free Trade party had gained its original purpose with the postponement of the effective date of nullification until after Congress had adjourned, and Virginia's intervention had enabled them to save face at the same time. The rank and file of the Unionists were less hostile as the end both parties sought seemed about to be achieved. The Force Bill, should it pass, would be another complication, but Calhoun's position was getting stronger every day. When men left their guns at home and concentrated their attention on the incoming mails, the danger of civil war was past.

ARTHUR M. SCHLESINGER, JR. (1917-   ) has placed himself at the head of those historians who find significant differences between the Jacksonians and their political opponents. His book on Jackson as well as his later works on the Age of Roosevelt establishes him as the nation's leading historian of American liberalism. The Jacksonians, he believes, wrought a peaceable revolution that they might preserve the reality of democracy in a changing economic and social order. They were no band of frontier radicals storming the strongholds of Eastern capitalism, for their ranks contained both farmers and urban workers from all sections. They fought entrenched capitalistic groups wherever such groups existed, making the conflict one of classes rather than sections.*

Jacksonian Democracy as an Intellectual Movement

The Jacksonian revolution rested on premises which the struggles of the thirties hammered together into a kind of practical social philosophy. The outline of this way of thinking about society was clear. It was stated and restated, as we have seen, on every level of political discourse from presidential messages to stump speeches, from newspaper editorials to private letters. It provided the intellectual background without which the party battles of the day cannot be understood.

1

The Jacksonians believed that there was a deep-rooted conflict in society between the "producing" and "non-producing" classes—the farmers and laborers, on the one hand, and the business community on the other. The business community was considered to hold high cards in this conflict through its network of banks and corporations, its control of education and the press, above all, its power over the state: it was therefore able to strip the working classes of the fruits of their labor. "Those who produce all wealth," said Amos Kendall, "are themselves left poor. They see principalities extending and palaces built around them, without being aware that the entire expense is a tax upon themselves."

If they wished to preserve their liberty,

* From Arthur M. Schlesinger, Jr., *The Age of Jackson.* Boston: Little Brown & Co., 1946. First published in 1945. Reprinted without footnotes by permission of the author.

the producing classes would have to unite against the movement "to make the rich richer and the potent more powerful." Constitutional prescriptions and political promises afforded no sure protection. "We have heretofore been too disregardful of the fact," observed William M. Gouge,* "that social order is quite as dependent on the laws which regulate the distribution of wealth, as on political organization." The program now was to resist every attempt to concentrate wealth and power further in a single class. Since free elections do not annihilate the opposition, the fight would be unceasing. "The struggle for power," said C. C. Cambreleng, "is as eternal as the division of society. A defeat cannot destroy the boundary which perpetually separates the democracy from the aristocracy."

The specific problem was to control the power of the capitalistic groups, mainly Eastern, for the benefit of the noncapitalist groups, farmers and laboring men, East, West and South. The basic Jacksonian ideas came naturally enough from the East, which best understood the nature of business power and reacted most sharply against it. The legend that Jacksonian democracy was the explosion of the frontier, lifting into the government some violent men filled with rustic prejudices against big business, does not explain the facts, which were somewhat more complex. Jacksonian democracy was rather a second American phase of that enduring struggle between the business community and the rest of society which is the guarantee of freedom in a liberal capitalist state.[1]

* Jacksonian editor, economist, and hard-money advocate—Ed.

[1] It may be well to observe contemporary apprehensions long enough to discuss the relationship of the Jacksonian analysis to Marxism.

Like any social philosophy, Jacksonian democracy drew on several intellectual traditions. Basically, it was a revival of Jeffersonianism, but the Jeffersonian inheritance was strengthened by the infusion of fresh influences; notably the antimonopolistic tradition, formulated primarily by Adam Smith and expounded in America by [William] Gouge, [William] Leggett, [Theodore] Sedgwick, Cambreleng; and the pro-labor tradition, formulated primarily by Wil-

Clarification would be useful, both for conservatives who declare that any talk of class conflict is Communistic, and for Communists who claim promiscuously any kind of economic insight as the exclusive result of their infallible method. In truth, the Jacksonian analysis, far from being Marxist, is the very core of our radical democratic tradition. The fact that the *Communist Manifesto* was not written until 1848 would seem conclusive on this point; and Marx and Lenin, unlike their disciples, made no irresponsible pretense to the invention of the theory of class conflict. Marx wrote to Weydemeyer, March 5, 1852: "As far as I am concerned, the honour does not belong to me for having discovered the existence either of classes in modern society or of the struggle between the classes. Bourgeois historians a long time before me expounded the historical development of this class struggle, and bourgeois economists, the economic anatomy of classes. What was new on my part, was to prove the following: (1) that the existence of classes is connected only with certain historical struggles which arise out of the development of production; (2) that class struggle necessarily leads to the dictatorship of the proletariat; (3) that this dictatorship is itself only a transition to the abolition of all classes and to a classless society."

Lenin is, if possible, more explicit. "The theory of the class struggle was *not* created by Marx, but by the bourgeoisie *before* Marx and is, generally speaking, *acceptable* to the bourgeoisie. He who recognizes *only* the class struggle is not yet a Marxist; he may be found not to have gone beyond the boundaries of bourgeois reasoning and politics. To limit Marxism to the teaching of the class struggle means to curtail Marxism—to distort it, to reduce it to something which is acceptable to the bourgeoisie. A Marxist is one who *extends* the acceptance of the class struggle to the acceptance of the *dictatorship of the proletariat*." V. I. Lenin, *State and Revolution* (New York, 1932), 29, 30.

liam Cobbett and expounded by G. H.
Evans, Ely Moore, John Ferral.**

2

The inspiration of Jeffersonianism
was so all-pervading and fundamental for
its every aspect that Jacksonian democracy can be properly regarded as a somewhat more hard-headed and determined
version of Jeffersonian democracy. But
it is easy to understate the differences.
Jefferson himself, though widely revered
and quoted, had no personal influence
on any of the leading Jacksonians save
perhaps Van Buren. Madison and Monroe were accorded still more vague and
perfunctory homage. The radical Jeffersonians, [John] Taylor, [John] Randolph and [Nathaniel] Macon, who had
regarded the reign of Virginia as almost
an era of betrayal, were much more
vivid in the minds of the Jacksonians.

Yet even Taylor's contributions to the
later period have been exaggerated. His
great work, the *Inquiry into the Principles and Policy of the Government of
the United States,* published in 1814 just
before the Madisonian surrender [to
Hamiltonian conservatism], had no significant contemporary vogue except
among the faithful; and its difficult
style, baffling organization and in-
terminable length prevented it ever from
gaining wide currency. By Jackson's
presidency it was long out of print. In
1835 it was reported unobtainable in
New York and to be procured only
"with great difficulty" in Virginia. There

** William Leggett was a Jacksonian editor;
Theodore Sedgwick, a New York lawyer and
author; William Cobbett, an English journalist
who was an admirer of Jackson; George H.
Evans, a New York editor and a leading advocate
of land reform as the solution to the workingman's problems; Ely Moore, a New York labor
leader and congressman; and John Ferral, a
Philadelphia labor leader—Ed.

is little trace of its peculiar terminology
in the Jacksonian literature.

While the *Inquiry* properly endured
as the most brilliant discussion of the
foundations of democracy, many of its
details were in fact obsolete by 1830. It
was oriented to an important degree
around the use of the national debt as
the mechanism of aristocracy; in Jackson's day the debt had been extinguished
but the aristocracy remained. Moreover,
Taylor's arguments against executive
power, against the party system and for
a revivified militia had lost their point
for the Jacksonians. George Bancroft
[the Massachusetts historian and Democratic party leader] voiced a widely felt
need when he called, in 1834, for a
general work on American society.
"Where doubts arise upon any point relating to the business of government,"
one radical wrote in response, "no dependence can be placed upon any trea-
tise that has yet appeared which professes
to discuss this subject. You must draw
upon your own resources, you must
think,—and think alone."

The obsolescence of Taylor was caused
by the enormous change in the face of
America. The period of conservative
supremacy from 1816 to 1828 had irrevocably destroyed the agricultural
paradise, and the Jacksonians were ac-
commodating the insights of Jefferson
to the new concrete situations. This
process of readjustment involved a mod-
erately thorough overhauling of favorite
Jeffersonian doctrines.

The central Jefferson hope had been
a nation of small freeholders, each acquiring thereby so much moral probity,
economic security and political independence as to render unnecessary any
invasion of the rights or liberties of
others. The basis of such a society, as
Jefferson clearly recognized, was agri-

culture and handicraft. What was the status of the Jeffersonian hope now that it was clear that, at best, agriculture must share the future with industry and finance?

Orestes A. Brownson [Boston author and editor] exhausted one possibility in his essay on "The Laboring Classes." He reaffirmed the Jeffersonian demand: "we ask that every man become an independent proprietor, possessing enough goods of this world, to be able by his own moderate industry to provide for the wants of his body." But what, in practice, would this mean? As Brownson acknowledged years later, his plan would have "broken up the whole modern commercial system, prostrated the great industries, . . . and thrown the mass of the people back on the land to get their living by agricultural and mechanical pursuits." Merely to state its consequences was to prove its futility. The dominion of the small freeholder was at an end.

The new industrialism had to be accepted: banks, mills, factories, industrial capital, industrial labor. These were all distasteful realities for orthodox Jeffersonians, and, not least, the propertyless workers. "The mobs of great cities," Jefferson had said, "add just so much to the support of pure government, as sores do to the strength of the human body." The very ferocity of his images expressed the violence of his feelings. "When we get piled upon one another in large cities, as in Europe," he told Madison, "we shall become corrupt as in Europe, and go to eating one another as they do there. It was a universal sentiment among his followers. "No man should live," Nathaniel Macon used to say, "where he can hear his neighbour's dog bark."

Yet the plain political necessity of winning the labor vote obliged a change of mood. Slowly, with some embarrassment, the Jeffersonian preferences for the common man were enlarged to take in the city workers. In 1833 the *New York Evening Post*, declaring that, if anywhere, a large city of mixed population would display the evils of universal suffrage, asked if this had been the case in New York and answered: No. Amasa Walker [Boston merchant, reformer, and radical Democrat] set out the same year to prove that "great cities are not *necessarily*, as the proverb says, 'great sores,'" and looked forward cheerily to the day when they would be "great fountains of healthful moral influence, sending forth streams that shall fertilize and bless the land." The elder Theodore Sedgwick added that the cause of the bad reputation of cities was economic: "it is the sleeping in garrets and cellars; the living in holes and dens; in dirty, unpaved, unlighted streets, without the accommodations of wells, cisterns, baths, and other means of cleanliness and health"— clear up this situation, and cities will be all right.

Jackson himself never betrayed any of Jefferson's revulsion to industrialism. He was, for example, deeply interested by the mills of Lowell in 1833, and his inquiries respecting hours, wages and production showed, observers reported, "that the subject of domestic manufactures had previously engaged his attentive observation." His presidential allusions to the "producing classes" always included the workingmen of the cities.

3

The acceptance of the propertyless laboring classes involved a retreat from one of the strongest Jeffersonian positions. John Taylor's distinction between "natural" and "artificial" property had enabled the Jeffersonians to enlist the moral and emotional resources contained in the notion of property. They could claim to be the protectors of property rights, while the business community, by despoiling the producers of the fruits of their labor, were the enemies of property. Yet, this distinction, if it were to have other than a metaphorical existence, had to rest on the dominance of agriculture and small handicraft. The proceeds of the labor of a farmer, or a blacksmith, could be measured with some exactness; but who could say what the "just" fruits of labour were for a girl whose labor consisted in one small operation in the total process of manufacturing cotton cloth? In what sense could propertyless people be deprived of their property?

Taylor had repeatedly warned that "fictitious" property would seek to win over "real" property by posing as the champion of all property against the mob. Now that the Democrats were the party, not only of small holders, but of propertyless workers, the conservative pose seemed more plausible. The Whigs diligently set forth to make every attack on "fictitious" capital an attack on all property rights. "The philosophy that denounces accumulation," said Edward Everett [leading Massachusetts Whig politician], "is the philosophy of barbarism." The outcry over monopoly, added Henry Clay, is "but a new form of attacking the rights of property. A man may not use his property in what form he pleases, even if sanctioned by the laws of the community in which he lives, without being denounced as a monopolist."

The Whigs slowly won the battle. The discovery of the courts that a corpora-

tion was really a person completed their victory. By 1843 William S. Wait [of Massachusetts] could strike the Jeffersonian flag: " 'Security to property' no longer means security to the citizen in the possession of his moderate competency, but security to him who monopolizes thousands—security to a few, who may live in luxury and ease upon the blood and sweat of many."

Jacksonians now tended to exalt human rights as a counterweight to property rights. The Whigs, charged Frank Blair, were seeking such an extension of "the rights of property as to swallow up and annihilate those of persons"; the Democratic party would "do all in its power to preserve and defend them." "We believe property should be held subordinate to man, and not man to property," said Orestes A. Brownson; "and therefore that it is always lawful to make such modifications of its constitution as the good of Humanity requires." The early decisions of Roger B. Taney's court helped establish the priority of the public welfare. But the Democrats had surrendered an important ideological bastion. The right to property provided a sturdy foundation for liberalism, while talk of human rights too often might end up in sentimentality or blood.

In several respects, then, the Jacksonians revised the Jeffersonian faith for America. They moderated that side of Jeffersonianism which talked of agricultural vitue, independent proprietors, "natural" property, abolition of industrialism, and expanded immensely that side which talked of economic equality, the laboring classes, human rights and the control of industrialism. This readjustment enabled the Jacksonians to attack economic problems which had baffled and defeated the Jeffersonians. It made for a greater realism, and was accompanied by a general toughening of the basic Jeffersonian conceptions. While the loss of "property" was serious, both symbolically and intellectually, this notion had been for most Jeffersonians somewhat submerged next to the romantic image of the free and virtuous cultivator; and the Jacksonians grew much more insistent about theories of capitalist alienation. Where, for the Jeffersonians, the tensions of class conflict tended to dissolve in vague generalizations about the democracy and the aristocracy, many Jacksonians would have agreed with A. H. Wood's remark, "It is in vain to talk of Aristocracy and Democracy—these terms are too variable and indeterminate to convey adequate ideas of the present opposing interests; the division is between the rich and the poor—the warfare is between them."

This greater realism was due, in the main, to the passage of time. The fears of Jefferson were now actualities. One handled fears by exorcism, but actualities by adjustment. For Jeffersonians mistrust of banks and corporations was chiefly a matter of theory; for the Jacksonians it was a matter of experience. The contrast between the scintillating metaphors of John Taylor and the sober detail of William M. Gouge expressed the difference. Jefferson rejected the Industrial Revolution and sought to perpetuate the smiling society which preceded it (at least, so the philosopher; facts compelled the President toward a different policy), while Jackson, accepting industrialism as an ineradicable and even useful part of the economic landscape, sought rather to control it. Jeffersonian democracy looked wistfully back toward a past slipping further every minute into the mists of memory, while Jacksonian democracy came straightfor-

wardly to grips with a rough and unlovely present.

The interlude saw also the gradual unfolding of certain consequences of the democratic dogma which had not been so clear to the previous generation. Though theoretically aware of the relation between political and economic power, the Jeffersonians had been occupied, chiefly, with establishing political equality. This was their mission, and they had little time to grapple with the economic questions.

But the very assertion of political equality raised inevitably the whole range of problems involved in property and class conflict. How could political equality mean anything without relative economic equality among the classes of the country? This question engaged the Jacksonians. As Orestes A. Brownson said, "A Loco-foco is a Jeffersonian Democrat, who having realized political equality, passed through one phase of the revolution, now passes on to another, and attempts the realization of social equality, so that the actual condition of men in society shall be in harmony with their acknowledged rights as citizens." This gap between Jeffersonian and Jacksonian democracy enabled men like John Quincy Adams, Henry Clay, Joseph Story and many others, who had been honest Jeffersonians, to balk at the economic extremities to which Jackson proposed to lead them.

The Jacksonians thus opened irrevocably the economic question, which the Jeffersonians had only touched half-heartedly. Yet, while they clarified these economic implications of democracy, the Jacksonians were no more successful than their predecessors in resolving certain political ambiguities. Of these, two were outstanding—the problem of the virtue of majorities, and the problem of the evil of government. Since the Jacksonians made useful explorations of these issues after 1840, they will be reserved for later discussion.

4

A second source of inspiration for the Jacksonians was the libertarian economic thought stirred up by Adam Smith and *The Wealth of Nations*. Believers in the myth of Adam Smith, as expounded by present-day publicists both of the right and of the left, may find this singular; but the real Adam Smith was rich in ammunition for the Jacksonians, as for any foe of business manipulation of the state.

The Weath of Nations quietly, precisely and implacably attacked the alliance of government and business, showing how monopoly retarded the economic growth of nations, and promoted the exploitation of the people. It was, in effect, a criticism of the kind of mercantilist policy which, in modified form, Hamilton had instituted in the Federalist program of the seventeen-nineties. Smith's classic argument against monopoly appealed strongly to the Jacksonians, and his distinction between productive and unproductive labor converged with the Jacksonian distinction between the producers and the nonproducers. They adopted his labor theory of value, in preference to the physiocratic doctrine which argued that value originated exclusively in land, and toward which Jefferson leaned. Smith's currency views were on the moderate hard-money line, favoring the suppression of notes under five pounds. And, contrary to the Adam Smith of folklore, the real Smith had no objection to government intervention which would protect, not exploit, the nation. "Those exertions of the natural liberty of a few individuals," he wrote, discussing the question of banking control, "which might endanger the security of the whole society, are, and ought to be, restrained by the laws of all governments; of the most free, as well as of the most despotical." His advocacy of education and his general hope for the well-being of the farming and laboring classes further recommended him to the Jacksonians.

In many respects, Adam Smith formulated on the economic level the same sentiments which Jefferson put into glowing moral and political language. Jefferson himself thought *The Wealth of Nations* "the best book extant" on economic questions. The translation of J. B. Say's popularization of Smith increased the currency of laissez faire doctrine. The little village of Stockbridge in Massachusetts was a particular center of free-trade thought. When Theodore Sedgwick observed of Adam Smith in 1838, "His voice has been ringing in the world's ears for sixty years, but it is only now in the United States that he is listened to, reverenced, and followed," the credit for this awakening went in great part to himself. His missionary efforts converted William Cullen Bryant, David Dudley Field and Theodore Sedgwick, Jr.,* and it was doubtless from Bryant that the previously nonpolitical Leggett got his introduction to *The Wealth of Nations*.

Leggett's brand of radicalism consisted almost entirely in a vigorous and unsparing effort to apply the doctrine of Adam Smith to the emerging corporate society. "If we analyze the nature and essence of free governments," Leggett wrote, "we

---

* All of New York. Bryant was an editor who is better remembered as a poet; Field and Sedgwick were lawyers. Field was a Van Buren lieutenant, Sedgwick a Democratic journalist— Ed.

shall find that they are more or less free in proportion to the absence of *monopolies*." From this central conviction stemmed his denunciation of the Bank, of the paper system and of the exclusive character of corporate grants. The *Evening Post* remained under Bryant's editorship the most consistently able organ of free-trade opinion. The radical wing of New York Democrats were the special advocates of *laissez faire*. C. C. Cambreleng, defending the Jacksonian program from the charge of agrarianism, once exclaimed indignantly in the House, "Were Franklin and Jefferson agrarians, sir? Was Adam Smith an agrarian?" Colonel Samuel Young [a Van Buren lieutenant and radical Democrat of New York] was a student of Smith and Say, as well as of Bentham, and the original Locofocos were free traders of the most doctrinaire sort.

The basic economic conception, which Adam Smith shared with Jefferson, was of a "natural order of things," that, once cleared of monopolistic clogs, would function to the greatest good of the greatest number. This conception, for all its apparent clarity, soon turned out to be packed with ambiguities. Free enterprise might mean, as with Leggett, a fighting belief in the virtue of competition, or it might mean, as with present-day conservatives, a fighting belief in the evil of government intervention. The battles of the Jackson era showed how these two interpretations of *laissez faire* were to come into increasing conflict.

The Jacksonians, vigorously in the first camp, had no hesitation in advocating government intervention in order to restore competition. In any case, their conception of the "natural order"—the region in which government was obligated not to interfere—included the right of the workingman to the full proceeds of his labor. Government, said Van Buren, should always be administered so as to insure to the laboring classes "a full enjoyment of the fruits of their industry."

Left to itself, and free from the blighting influence of partial legislation, monopolies, congregated wealth, and interested combinations, the compensation of labor will always preserve this salutary relation. It is only when the natural order of society is disturbed by one or other of these causes, that the wages of labor become inadequate.

The prescription of free enterprise thus became government action to destroy the "blighting influence of partial legislation, monopolies, congregated wealth, and interested combinations" in the interests of the "natural order of society."

But the language of Adam Smith, as a result of its origin in a critique of mercantilism as government policy, lent itself also to attacks on government intervention. The presidency of Jackson had begun to reduce the conservative enthusiasm, in the manner of Hamilton, for state interference, and the business community commenced now to purloin the phrases of *laissez faire*. By 1888 E. M. Shepard, a Grover Cleveland Democrat, could dedicate a biography of Van Buren to the thesis that Van Buren was a thoroughgoing foe of government intervention—a thesis which required the total omission of such measures as the order establishing the ten-hour day.

In the end, business altogether captured the phrases of *laissez faire* and used them more or less ruthlessly in defense of monopoly, even coupling them with arguments for the protective tariff, a juxtaposition which would at least have given earlier conservatives a decent sense of embarrassment. Adam Smith himself doubted whether large businessmen really believed in free competition. The sequel confirmed his doubts. The irony was that the slogans of free trade, which he developed in order to destroy monopoly, should end up as its bulwark.

5

A third important stimulus to the Jacksonians was the foaming tide of social revolt in Britain, reaching them primarily through the writings of William Cobbett. As the "Peter Porcupine" of Federalist journalism, Cobbett had been an early object of Jeffersonian wrath. But, on returning to Britain after some years in America, Cobbett discovered that the conservative values he had been so stalwartly defending were rapidly disappearing before the smokey ravages of industrialism. He gave splendid and angry expression to the hatred of independent workingmen for the impending degradation, and his fluent, robust, abusive prose created a new political consciousness among the common people of Britain.

A vehement advocate of the rights of workers to the full fruits of their industry, and a savage enemy of the new financial aristocracy, he found a rapt audience in America, especially in the labor movement. *Paper against Gold,* reprinted in New York in 1834, helped the hard-money campaign. William H. Hale of New York, the author of *Useful Knowledge for the Producers of Wealth,* and Thomas Brothers, the editor of the *Radical Reformer* of Philadelphia, were perhaps his leading disciples, but his unquenchable vitality inspired the whole radical wing.

Cobbett on his part watched events across the Atlantic with immense enthusiasm. Jackson's fight against the Bank stirred him to the inordinate conclusion that Jackson was "the bravest and greatest man now living in this world, or that ever has lived in this world, as far as my knowledge extends." He wrote a life of Jackson (or rather interpolated characteristic comments into a reprint of Eaton's book, and even issued an abridged version of Gouge's *Paper Money,* under the title of *The Curse of Paper-Money and Banking.* He addressed superb open letters to the American President, and his admiration for "the greatest soldier and the greatest statesman whose name has ever yet appeared upon the records of valour and of wisdom" never faltered.

Yet, with all his passion for social justice, Cobbett talked very little about democracy. He seemed almost to feel— and his American followers had similar overtones—that, if the speculators, rag barons and capitalists were thrown out, and the lower classes instituted in power, the main problems of society would be solved. His gusty idealization of the British yeoman, redolent of beef and beer, led him away from theories of class balance into implications of class infallibility, almost at times leaning from democracy toward socialism. These were but shadings, and in his American disciples shades of shadings. Yet George H. Evans, John Commerford [of New York], John Ferral and the early labor leaders seemed to regard democracy as more protective doctrine than good in itself. In power they might have acted little differently—if toward different ends—from Daniel Webster and Nicholas Biddle.

6

The radical democrats had a definite conception of their relation to history. From the Jeffersonian analysis, fortified by the insights of Adam Smith and Cobbett, they sketched out an interpretation of modern times which gave meaning and status to the Jacksonian struggles.

Power, said the Jacksonians, goes with property. In the Middle Ages the feudal nobility held power in society through its monopoly of land under feudal tenure. The overthrow of feudalism, with the rise of new forms of property, marked the first step in the long march toward freedom. The struggle was carried on by the rising business community—"Commercial, or business capital, against landed capital; merchants, traders, manufacturers, artizans, against the owners of the soil, the great landed nobility." It lasted from the close of the twelfth century to the Whig Revolution of 1688 in Britain.

The aristocracy of capital thus destroyed the aristocracy of land. The business classes here performed their vital role in the drama of liberty. The victory over feudalism, as the *Democratic Review* put it, "opened the way for the entrance of the democratic principle into the Government." But the business community gained from this exploit an undeserved reputation as the champion of liberty. Its real motive had been to establish itself in power, not to free mankind; to found government on property, not on the equal rights of the people. "I know perfectly well what I am saying," cried George Bancroft, "and I assert expressly, and challenge contradiction, that in all the history of the world there is not to be found an instance of a commercial community establishing rules for self-government upon democratic principles." "It is a mistake to suppose commerce favorable to liberty," added Fenimore Cooper. "Its tendency is to a monied aristocracy." "Instead of setting man free," said Amos Kendall, it has "only increased the number of his masters."

The next great blow for liberty was the American Revolution, "affected not in favor of men in classes; . . . but in favor of men." But the work of Hamilton halted the march of democracy. "He established the money power," wrote Van Buren, "upon precisely the same foundations upon which it had been raised in England." The subsequent history of the United States was the struggle to overthrow the Hamiltonian policy and fulfill the ideals of the Revolution.

What of the future? The Jacksonians were sublimely confident: history was on their side. "It is now for the yeomanry and the mechanics to march at the head of civilization," said Bancroft. "The merchants and the lawyers, that is, the moneyed interest broke up feudalism. The day for the multitude has now dawned." "All classes, each in turn, have possessed the government," exclaimed Brownson; "and the time has come for all predominance of class to end; for Man, the People to rule."

This was not simply a national movement. It was a movement of all people, everywhere, against their masters, and the Jacksonians watched with keen interest the stirrings of revolt abroad. Jackson and his cabinet joined in the celebrations in Washington which followed the Revolution of 1830 in France; and Van Buren, as Secretary of State, ordered the new government informed that the American people were "universally and enthusiastically in favor of that change, and of the principle upon which it was effected." (The Whigs, on the other hand, in spite of Clay's support of national revolutions in Greece and South America, remained significantly lukewarm.) Lamennais, the eloquent voice of French popular aspirations, was read in Jacksonian circles. The *Paroles d'un Croyant* influenced Orestes A. Brownson, and in 1839 *Le Livre du Peuple* was published in Boston under the title of *The People's Own Book,* translated by Nathaniel Greene, postmaster of Boston, brother of Charles Gordon Greene of the *Post* and intimate of David Henshaw [Massachusetts businessman, politician, and Democratic party leader].

Democrats followed with similar enthusiasm the progress of the Reform Bill in England, while the Whigs sympathized with the Tories. The Chartist uprisings at the end of the decade were greeted with delight by the Democratic press. British reformers returned this interest. Not only Cobbett and Savage Landor but the veteran radical Jeremy Bentham observed Jackson's administration with approval. Bentham, a friend of John Quincy Adams, had been disappointed at the triumph in 1828 of this military hero; but early in 1830, as he huddled by his hissing steam radiator, he heard read aloud Jackson's first message to Congress. The old man was highly pleased to discover greater agreement with the new President than with the old. Later he wrote that lengthy and cryptic memorandum entitled *Anti-Senatica,* intended to aid Jackson in the problems of his administration.

Jacksonians everywhere had this faith in the international significance of their fight. For this reason, as well as from a desire to capture their votes, Democratic leaders made special appeals to newly naturalized citizens. Where many Whigs tended to oppose immigration and demand sanctions against it, Democrats welcomed the newcomers with open arms and attacked the nativist agitation. The United States must remain a refuge from tyranny. "The capitalist class," said Samuel J. Tilden [of New York], "has banded together all over the world and organized the *modern dynasty of associated wealth,* which maintains an unquestioned ascendency over most of the civilized portions of our race." America was the proving-ground of democracy, and it was the mission of American Democrats to exhibit to the world the glories of government by the people. They were on the spearhead of history. They would not be denied. "With the friends of freedom throughout the world," declared Theophilus Fisk,* "let us be co-workers." "The People of the World," cried Fanny Wright,** "have but one Cause."

* New England journalist and advocate of the workingman's cause—Ed.
** The fascinating, unpredictable, Scotch-born reformer who advocated various radical causes—Ed.

EDWARD PESSEN (1920-   ) belongs to a group of
historians, generally identified with Columbia
University, who criticize Schlesinger's interpretation
of Jacksonian Democracy, especially his views on the
crucial role played by labor in the movement. Joseph
Dorfman, a leader of this group, denies that the
labor spokesmen cited by Schlesinger were antibusiness,
nor does he consider them representatives of a
genuine labor movement. Richard Morris, also a
Schlesinger critic, maintains that Jackson was
antilabor. Pessen, in the selection below, does not
support either of these interpretations completely,
but he does deny that the labor movement was
anticapitalist and that it was associated closely with
the Democratic party.*

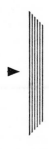

The Workingmen's Movement
of the Jacksonian Era

In the eleven years since the publication of *The Age of Jackson,* by Arthur
M. Schlesinger, Jr., as the interest of
students of the Jacksonian era has been
turned to a closer examination of the
social complexion and ideology of the
reform movement which allegedly co-
alesced around the person and the program of President Jackson, important
questions have been raised about the
labor movement of that period. On the
one hand, Joseph Dorfman, challenging
what he calls the Jackson wage-earner
thesis, has questioned both the authenticity of the movement and the radicalism and anticapitalism attributed to its
leaders.[1] On the other hand, the long-
popular thesis that eastern workingmen
constituted an important part of the
Jacksonian coalition and that their votes
were instrumental in Jackson's political
victories has also come under serious
criticism. Recent studies have shown
that urban workers, organized and unorganized, often voted against Jackson
and candidates supporting him.[2] This
conclusion, when complemented by

[1] Joseph Dorfman, "The Jackson Wage-Earner
Thesis," *American Historical Review* (New York),
LIV (January, 1949), 296-306.
[2] William A. Sullivan, "Did Labor Support
Andrew Jackson?" *Political Science Quarterly*
(New York), LXII (December, 1947), 569-80;
Edward Pessen, "Did Labor Support Jackson?
The Boston Story," *ibid.,* LXIV (June, 1949),
262-74; Milton J. Nadworny, "Jersey Labor and
Jackson" (M.A. thesis, Columbia University,
1948).

* Edward Pessen, "The Workingmen's Movement of the Jacksonian Era," *The Mississippi Valley Historical Review,* XLIII (December 1956). Most of the footnotes that accompanied the article as originally published have been omitted by permission.

proof that Jackson was a "strike-breaker,"[3] suggests not only that Old Hickory was no friend to the working-man and that the fact was known to them, but further that pro-Jackson parties or movements professing to represent the workers actually did not do so.

The purpose of this paper is to throw light on the actual character of the movement of the late 1820's and the 1830's, which until recently had been widely regarded as America's first real labor movement,[4] by attempting to answer certain basic questions relating to it. Was the movement authentic—that is, was it composed of bona fide wage earners battling in the interests of wage earners; or was it spurious, consisting instead of wily politicians who wrapped themselves in the "workingmen's" mantle only to hide their real nature? Were the movement and its leaders radical, or in any sense anti-capitalistic? What was the relationship of this movement of wage earners to the broader program of the Democratic party, which had attracted men of widely varying social classes and ideologies?

The alleged labor groups which emerged in the large eastern cities during this period assumed a variety of forms. Workingmen's parties, trade societies of individual crafts, trades unions, associations of urban and rural artisans and workers, national unions in a few select crafts, and one short-lived "National Trades' Union," were established, only to disappear or to merge into one another. Certainly the character of these organizations is to be determined neither by accepting their own assertions at face value nor by considering them uncritically as equally representative examples of an actual labor movement, but rather by careful examination of the evidence relating to each of them.

In Philadelphia, the Mechanics' Union of Trade Associations was organized late in 1827, growing out of a strike by the journeymen carpenters for the ten-hour day. This "first union of all the organized workmen of any city" was formed by journeymen bricklayers, painters, glaziers, typographers, and members of other trade societies sympathetic to the carpenters. The journeymen carpenters held a meeting on July 1, 1828, at which plans were made to secure the nomination of candidates who would "support the interests of the working classes." Thus was born the Working Men's party of Philadelphia, in the promise by some workingmen to support at the polls individuals sympathetic to the needs of workers. Although the party flourished for only one year and then went into a steady decline until its demise in 1832, a great deal has been written about it. It has been shown that it was not heavily supported by workingmen at the polls, that it nominated many wealthy merchants to office, that it was eventually infiltrated by opportunistic political elements which brought about its ruin, and that throughout its history it favored a very general program of humanitarian reform. Yet it also clearly championed the cause of labor by advocating the ten-hour day and by continuing the agitation begun earlier by individual trade societies for a mechanics' lien law, and it was

---

[3] Richard B. Morris, "Andrew Jackson, Strike-breaker," *American Historical Review,* LV (October, 1949), 54-68.

[4] In his classic history of labor, John R. Commons called the formation of trades unions and workingmen's parties, first in Philadelphia in 1827, followed soon by like developments in New York, Boston, Newark, and Baltimore, the first American labor movement, because "American wage-earners for the first time joined together as a class, regardless of trade lines, in a contest with employers." John R. Commons and Associates, *History of Labour in the United States* (2 vols., New York, 1918), I, 25, 169.

at first independent of the major parties. If it supported non-workingmen for office it was only living up to the promise, made by the journeymen workers who organized the party, to judge candidates by their policies rather than their social backgrounds. And in favoring such reforms as abolition of imprisonment for debt, a more democratic militia system, and free public schools, the Philadelphia party, like workingmen's parties elsewhere, was expressing not its non-wage-earner character but rather the great interest felt by American wage earners in the democratization of American society and the curbing of abuses whose burdens fell most heavily on the shoulders of workingmen. American workmen, like Americans of other social groupings, were concerned with many issues seemingly not directly related to the economic interests of their "class." Men then as now lived not by bread alone.

After the decline of the political movement, Philadelphia journeymen organized a number of trades unions in the early and middle 1830's. These unions comprised thousands of workers, and their outstanding achievement was a successful strike for a ten-hour working day in 1835. There can be little question of the legitimacy of these aggressive organizations which exerted continual pressure for better conditions and shorter working hours.

The authenticity of the New York Working Men's party has also been questioned. Like its Philadelphia counterpart the New York City party underwent strange and checkered experiences, but these do not erase the indisputable evidence of its ties and sympathies with bona fide workingmen. The party grew out of a movement to protect the ten-hour day. Its actual birth took place on

April 23, 1829, when a meeting of mechanics and others, who had gathered to protest against extension of working hours, voted to form a political party in order to attain this and other objectives. The party conferred leadership on a Committee of Fifty, composed largely of workers in the building trades, a group whose radicalism is attested by its opposition both to the membership of "bosses" in the party and to the principle of private property in society. Through its newspaper, *The Working Man's Advocate,* the party displayed its support not only of humanitarian reform, but of trades, unions, strikes, and the interests of journeymen workers as well. Though Thomas Skidmore, the party's early leader, had some notions which might seem conservative when they are isolated from his total program, he nevertheless believed that only workingmen and the poor should play a part in the organization and his over-all social outlook was markedly radical.

After its first political success in the elections of November, 1829, when it elected one and came near electing several others of its candidates to local office, the party was overwhelmed with difficulties. It was beset by factionalism, invaded by non-labor schemers and opportunists, allowed itself to be dominated either by conservatives or by doctrinaire individuals neither of whom represented actual workingmen, and after two short years it skidded into oblivion. But the pains taken by non-labor elements to infiltrate and dominate the new organization were testimony to its early character and effectiveness as a labor body. The party made many mistakes and was frequently led by impractical theorists, but these failings indicate human frailty rather than fraudulent misrepresentation.

As was the case elsewhere, New York

City experienced a vigorous trades-union movement in the years before the Panic of 1837. Its General Trades' Union, formed in August, 1833, as a result of a journeymen carpenters' strike for higher wages was composed of journeymen workers in many trades, ranging from leather dressers to cabinetmakers. Its strikes for higher wages and better working conditions would seem to establish its authenticity as a labor organization.

Varied labor organizations also arose in New England. In Boston a workingmen's party was formed in August, 1830. It was a rather broad organization which resolved to exclude "none who by their honest industry render an equivalent to society for the means of subsistence which they draw therefrom." In common with other workingmen's parties the Boston group nominated many wealthy men to office and supported an all-embracing reform program. Among its demands, however, were better conditions for laborers. Though it was a timid rather than an aggressive organization, its very existence exasperated that section of the business community which liked to think that merchants and capitalists, too, were workingmen.

More significant than this party was the "New England Association for Farmers, Mechanics, and other Working Men," an interesting organization which concerned itself with many other matters besides labor activities, and in which a number of Democratic politicians were active. The Association, which was born at Providence, Rhode Island, in December, 1831, and died less than three years later at Northampton, Massachusetts, was not quite in fact what its name proclaimed it to be. Its own convention proceedings show clearly that farmers and factory workers, though the source of much discussion, where not drawn into

the organization in any significant numbers. But there are important signs that it was nevertheless a bona fide labor organization. The evidence indicates that Boston journeymen ship carpenters, who planned to strike for a ten-hour day on March 20, 1832—the very date of the Association's first convention, in Boston—played an important role at that gathering. The constitution formulated at the convention provided not only for support of the ten-hour day but also for the raising of a war chest to finance the strike. At ensuing conventions the Association discussed numerous issues, some of which had little to do with labor, supported some opportunistic political candidates, and in general comported itself like what in fact it was—a movement which had neither a hard and fast practical program nor social philosophy. Yet it regularly recommended the establishment of trades unions, desired the organization of a national union, and attacked the operation of the factory system. In it such leading trades-union figures as Seth Luther, Charles Douglas, and John Ferral played active roles. It was an excellent example of the breadth of interest of American workingmen of the era, and of their hope, impractical though it was, that all men who performed useful labor might be brought together into one organization.

In March, 1834, a trades union was organized in Boston, in accord with resolutions passed at the 1833 convention of the New England Association. Unlike the unions in the other major cities, the Boston union did not confine itself to matters of wages and hours but also took strong stands on political questions and the broad range of issues which earlier had concerned the workingmen's parties. It went under in 1835 after still another strike for the ten-hour day by the journeymen carpenters, masons, stonecutters, and housewrights failed.

The Philadelphia, New York, and New England groups were similar to the numerous other labor organizations which sprang up in northeastern cities during this period. They were unlike the unions of today which have a more or less similar range of union activities and job objectives. What has been called the labor movement of the period from 1827 to 1837 consisted of varied organizations with all-embracing social programs. In their complexity and scope they reflected the situation and the mood of the American workman of that era: a man who while a worker today might become a master tomorrow; a man who dreamed of ascending into a higher social stratum as he simultaneously demanded the right to organize and to strike. Its unique characteristics notwithstanding, a labor movement made up of genuine labor organizations did in fact exist during the Age of Jackson.

The next question concerns the ideology of the movement and its leaders. Their writings and speeches might be expected to show whether their viewpoint reflected a spirit of radicalism and anticapitalism which was not in accord with the general philosophy of the "Jacksonian reform movement" as a whole. Did they, for example, express points of view hostile to, or sharply critical of, or favoring drastic changes in a private-enterprise society's fundamental institutions? In making such an examination it is necessary to recognize the difference between those reform leaders of the period who did not concern themselves directly with labor questions and those who may be considered as leaders in the labor movement. Obviously, such prominent reform figures, for example, as Theodore Sedgwick, William M. Gouge,

Condy Raguet, or Samuel Clesson Allen, whatever they may have been, were not labor leaders. Nor would reformers, or faddists, or politicians qualify as labor leaders, even by the broader standards of that time, merely because they supported Jackson or because they occasionally agreed with a labor representative or happened to share a platform with him. Since a labor movement consisting of specific organizations did exist, only those men who had more or less direct ties with these labor organizations may properly be classified as labor leaders.

The early labor leaders were as diverse as the movement they represented, both in their backgrounds and in the nature of their affiliation to labor organizations. Some of them, such as George Henry Evans and Robert Dale Owen of the New York Working Men's party, Stephen Simpson, political candidate of the Philadelphia workingmen, and Theophilus Fisk, active in New England labor groups, were essentially middle-class reformers who had only brief ties with labor groups, and primarily with those of a political nature. Thomas Skidmore, who dominated the early New York labor party, was an unusually well—if self-educated machinist. Thomas Brothers, who published a labor weekly in Philadelphia during the days of the ten-hour movement, was actually a small capitalist whose hat-making establishment bore most of the advertising load of his journal. Even such trades-union leaders as John Commerford, Ely Moore, and Levi D. Slamm in New York, Seth Luther and Charles Douglas in Boston, and John Ferral and William English in Philadelphia, were not all actual workingmen. Moore, Slamm, English, and, to a lesser extent, Douglas clearly regarded their labor activities as possible springboards to successful political careers. Yet each of them was active in behalf of one or more bona fide labor organizations. In labor journals, pamphlets, books, addresses to workingmen, and open letters, each of these leaders presented his own social philosophy, or his indictment of the contemporary scene. No such group could be expected to agree in all particulars, and these did not. Yet, despite the variations in their backgrounds and motives, the thought of these men, who provide a representative cross section of the leadership of the early northeastern labor movement, is nevertheless strikingly uniform.

When their social philosophies are brought together and studied, the composite analysis seems to show that labor leaders of the Jackson period were generally agreed that American society was marred by the existence of poverty and misery on a large scale. On one side, they said, were the idle rich and the capitalists, living in a splendor derived from the poverty of the many, while on the other were the laboring poor who lived in squalor. What was especially provoking about this unhappy development was that, paradoxically, it was occurring at a time when the economy was becoming increasingly productive, and when the rule therefore should have been "plenty for all." This situation persisted, it was maintained, because all the strategic institutions of American life, particularly the political, were controlled by the wealthy classes, who frankly used their power to perpetuate their dominance. Contending that society was shot through with tension caused by the conflicting interests of classes, these labor leaders warned the workingmen against permitting themselves to be beguiled into denying the existence of this conflict. The rich and the capitalists, they said, were aware of social war but denied its

existence only in order that they might wage it more effectively.

According to the labor leaders, the rise of democracy had not relieved the plight of the workingmen. It had merely made it necessary for the leading parties to exercise all their wiles in order to delude the workingmen into accepting and supporting a scheme based on their own subordination. The political parties had proved equal to the occasion and now said the labor spokesmen, it was time for workingmen to realize that their interests as a class were distinct and were not to be advanced by depending on the disinterestedness of those who were plundering them.

Of primary importance to the leaders of the labor movement was what they called the degradation of labor. They charged that although they alone created all wealth, workingmen were denied even a reasonable share of society's product. Laborers not only worked long hours for low wages under bad working conditions, but they were also held in low esteem by their fellow men. In answer to the explanation often given that workingmen were culturally inferior, it was claimed that their apparent inferiority flowed from their inadequate opportunity to participate in cultural activities— they had not the income, the leisure, nor the taste for them.

What accounted for the misery of labor as well as the other gloomy conditions characteristic of contemporary society? Various factors were held responsible. Malthusianism and other explanations which attributed man's difficulties either to man's depravity or to immutable laws of political economy were rejected as rationalizations for the rich. Social distress was not due to man's own innate shortcomings; it was caused by asocial institutions. Monopolies, most banking operations, paper money, private property, machines, and a factory system dominated by selfish men were among the factors held responsible for social injustice. Emphases varied within this framework according to the individual. Skidmore's interpretation of the evils of private property was more drastic than that of his American if not his English labor colleagues. In the debate on machines and the factory system, attitudes ranged from their outright rejection and denunciation to support based on the anticipation that machinery would one day lighten the burden for all workers.

Labor leaders almost invariably regarded the future with optimism. Domination of the poor by the rich was believed to be a violation of natural rights and the natural order, which would triumph in the end. It was held that despite flaws grafted in his personality and character by the allegedly vicious social environment in which he lived man was still capable of bringing about the Good Society. Opinions varied, however, on the nature of the Good Society which would eventually prevail. Most of the leaders seemed to favor a kind of socialism in which each person was rewarded by society according to how much he had contributed to it in labor. Nearly all hoped that there would be social equality and that workingmen would come into their own, with respect both to status and to material conditions.

Means for the achievement of the ideal society were also varied. Popular education belonged high on the list. An educated working class, it was believed, would know how to take the steps necessary for the reform of society. On the other hand a few of the leaders felt that too much was being made of education by those who had an aversion for more drastic methods of instituting reform. The way to thoroughgoing reform, it was held, lay in political action. Many

labor leaders believed that unless such reform were forthcoming a revolution would soon develop, blame for which would fall squarely on the wealthy. Though a number of the leaders seemed to regard a revolution with no disapproval, only one of them, Thomas Skidmore, actually advocated a revolution— to be carried through peaceably by the majority of the population. And of course to supplement political action workers must also organize strong and aggressive trades unions. One thing was certainly very clear in their thinking. The way to social justice was not in the patient wait for benevolence from above. Instead, workingmen had to take matters into their own hands and by one means or another bring about a society organized around the principle that no class deserved more than those who labored.

These, in sum, were the social ideas of the labor leaders of the period. Their image of America, it hardly needs saying, seems one-sided and overdrawn. Businessmen, journalists, and foreign travelers among their contemporaries saw an altogether different social landscape, marked by comparative equality and widespread abundance. As was true of reformers in other fields, these labor leaders concentrated on the seamy side of contemporary conditions. By doing so they reveal not so much the actual state of society as their own radical state of mind. Social programs which assume class conflict, the domination of society by a few wealthy capitalists, the wickedness of private property and the necessity of fundamental change along socialist lines are properly described as radical or anticapitalistic. Whether all of the leaders actually believed that the picture was as somber as they painted it, is hard to determine. What is important, however, was their willingness, publicly, to stand behind and be judged by these radical professions.

With respect to the question of the relationship, if any, between the labor movement and the broad Jacksonian political coalition, it should be clear that they were two different things. The various workingmen's organizations of that era were formed not to achieve the objectives of the Democratic party but to find the solution to workingmen's problems. Though the labor groups occasionally supported one or another of the Jacksonian policies, they did not thereby merge with the broader movement, nor did they lose their identity or become mere appendages of the Democratic party. The essential independence of the early labor movement from the Jacksonian cause is illustrated not alone by how labor voted but also by the uniquely radical doctrines of its leaders, even with respect to those issues on which Jacksonian reformers held somewhat similar positions.

Education was such an issue. The labor leaders, in common with other Americans, supported a system of free public education. However, while liberals anticipated the regeneration of man and perhaps the harmonizing of the discordant interests in society as the happy consequences of universal schooling, and while conservatives looked forward to its happy effects in turning workingmen away from iniquitous reform doctrines, labor hoped for quite different results. Labor leaders supported universal public education because it would enable labor to "remove the veil of ignorance by which the poor who suffer are prevented from penetrating into the mysteries of the rich by which their sufferings are produced." An educated working class would remove those politicians who represented "interests opposed to those of the working men," and replace them with workers, who would pass "just laws, such as [would] defend their rights and advance their interests." (It was because they knew and feared this, labor leaders said, that capitalists threw up obstacles to mass education.) Mass education would lead to greater social equality and put an end to capitalistic abuses. Finally, it was in the education of the working class and in its knowledge of the fundamental truths of society, including its own true worth, that were contained the hopes for the soltuion to society's major problems. It is apparent that the labor leaders anticipated advantages to be derived from public education that were not dreamed of by other supporters of the public school system, namely, the awakening of workingmen to their own true interests, as well as the means for their realization.

The labor leaders' views on the related issues of monoply, banking, and paper currency are also worthy of closer study. Though they shared the attitudes of such Jacksonian reformers as Clinton Roosevelt [a New York radical Democrat], Theodore Sedgwick, Jr., John W. Vethake [a physician and occasional contributor to the *New York Evening Post*], William Leggett, and William M. Gouge about the perfidy of these institutions, labor's position was distinct from and more radical than that of these theorists and pamphleteers. The labor leaders attacked monopolistic powers conferred by legislatures on private corporations well before the issue became a standard one with the liberal wing of Democrats or the "Friends of Equal Rights." Even when the labor leaders and Jacksonian reformers agreed in attacking monopoly, they differed in their reasoning. Labor was concerned over the tendency of the monopolistic system to "defraud labor," while the laissez faire Jacksonians complained rather of the restraints it imposed on less favored entrepreneurs.

The labor leaders' assault on banking and paper money was by no means an exact replica of the middle-class reformers' criticism of these institutions. To the "anti-monopolists" the main objection to the banking system was the fact that it was controlled by an aristocratic few and was not sufficiently open to the participation of the entire community; but the labor spokesmen opposed banking as such. In their view, bankers lived off labor, and the paper money they issued was a fraud which inevitably depreciated the real value of the workers' earnings.

Perhaps the clearest evidence of the independent attitude of the early labor leaders toward the Jacksonian political movement is afforded by their comment on politics. Almost all of them believed that both the political system in general and the major parties in particular benefited the wealthy classes at the expense of the workingmen. According to to them, politics was simply another facet through which was expressed the class antagonism rending society, and the major parties simply instruments of plunder. Nor did they confine such talk to generalities. Douglas advised a workingmen's convention that the "working class . . . belonged to no party; they were neither disciples of Jacksonism nor Clayism, Van Burenism nor Websterism, nor any other ism but workeyism," Evans was thrilled that the spokesmen of the workingmen's parties "renounced all connexion with every party . . . and that they are decidedly opposed to coalition." Commerford warned the workingmen that it was "useless for [them] to rely on either party for the advancement of [their] rights." The major parties were frauds: "Stand aloof, remember we have no alliance with either of the humbugs,"

he concluded. Ferral hoped that workers would no longer be "duped" by the lawmakers of either party. English spoke contemptuously of the habit of both parties to feign interest in the workingmen's problems only as election day neared. The Democrats, like their "aristocratic" opponents, served the interests of the bankers and monopolists, according to Brothers, the only difference being that their leaders masked an identification that the Whigs were frank to proclaim. Nor were such criticisms atypical. Rather they were representative of a persistent denunciation by labor spokesmen of the party system of their era.

What is to be concluded concerning the relationship between this early labor movement, led by radicals who often sharply criticized the Democratic party, and Jacksonian democracy? To the extent that it, too, opposed aristocratic privilege and monoply, the labor movement may be interpreted as part of a broadly defined "Jacksonian Revolution"; but neither the organized labor movement nor unorganized workingmen became a fixed part of a Democratic political coalition. [And if the Jacksonian movement was in fact a movement primarily devoted to achieving a freer competitive capitalism, workingmen certainly had demands which went far beyond that objective. Yet according to the large view which seeks to impose a pattern on an era, reforms of varied character, championed by diverse groups, each seeking the achievement of its separate objectives, nevertheless merge together in a broad, all-embracing reform movement. It is only in this general sense that the American labor organizations of the Jacksonian era can be said to have been a part of a large, sweeping movement, toward whose political expression—the Democratic party—they often displayed indifference if not actual hostility.

BRAY HAMMOND (1886-   ) has launched an attack
on Schlesinger's interpretation of the Jacksonian
opposition to the national bank, first in a review
of the *Age of Jackson* and later in an article,
both published in the *Journal of Economic History*
(1946 and 1947). His book, from which the
following section is taken, amplified and
documented his charges and developed his
"entrepreneural" thesis. The Jacksonian revolution,
declared Hammond, placed in power a group of
incipient entrepreneurs who employed agrarian
ideology to accomplish nonagrarian objectives.
The bank was destroyed because its power to regulate
credit posed a threat to the Jacksonians in reaching
their objectives.*

The Jacksonians

I

During the half century that ended
with General Jackson's election, America
underwent changes perhaps the most
radical and sweeping it has ever under-
gone in so short a time. It passed the
climacteric separating a modern industrial economy from an older one of
handicraft; it passed from colonial weakness through bare independence to actual
power and from an unjostled rural
culture to the complexities of populous-
ness, sectionalism, urban slums, mechan-
ized industry, and monetary credit. Men
who had spent their childhood in a thin
line of sea-board colonies, close even in
their little cities to the edge of the west-

ward continental wilderness, spent their
late years in a tamed and wealthy land
spread already to the Missouri and about
to extend beyond it. They lived to ride
on railways and steamships, to use the
products of steam-driven machinery, to
dwell in metropolitan centers, and to
feel within their grasp and the grasp of
their sons more potential and accessible
wealth than had ever before excited the
enterprise of man.

An outstanding factor in the changes
that came about was the flow of immigration from Europe. Between 1790 and
1840 the population grew from 4,000,000
to 17,000,000. In the latter year an average of 230 immigrants entered the

country daily. Ten years later it was over 1,000 daily. The area of settlement and exploitation expanded swiftly under the pressure of this movement. While General Jackson was President the federal union came to include twice as many states as it had begun with and held territory that recently had belonged to Spain and France. It was shortly to add regions in the South and West taken from Mexico and regions in the Northwest that Great Britain claimed. Its expansion seemed irresistible.

The changes in social outlook were profound. Steam was generating conceptions of life, liberty, and the pursuit of happiness that were quite alien to Thomas Jefferson's; and the newcomers pushing into the country from Europe had more impatient economic motives than their 18th century predecessors. People were led as they had not been before by visions of money-making. Liberty became transformed into *laisser faire.* A violent, aggressive, economic individualism became established. The democracy became greedy, intolerant, imperialistic, and lawless. It opened economic advantages to those who had not previously had them; yet it allowed wealth to be concentrated in new hands only somewhat more numerous than before, less responsible, and less disciplined. There were unenterprising and unpropertied thousands who missed entirely the economic opportunities with which America was thick. There was poverty in the eastern cities and poverty on the frontier. Those who failed to hold their own in the struggle were set down as unfit.

Wealth was won and lost, lost and won. Patient accumulation was contemned. People believed it was not what they saved but what they made that counted. ... Something of the same

sort, to be sure, was taking place in western Europe and especially in Great Britain. Half the people and most of the money for America's transformation came from there. But though industrial and technological revolution occurred also in the Old World, in the New, where vast resources awaited exploitation, it produced a dazzling, democratic expansion experienced nowhere else. The situation was such that the rallying cry, *"Laissez nous faire!"* expressed the views of Americans perfectly, when translated.

Socially, the Jacksonian revolution signified that a nation of democrats was tired of being governed, however well, by the gentlemen from Virginia and Massachusetts. As Professor [William Graham] Sumner observed, what seems to have enchanted people with General Jackson when he became a candidate for President was not any principles or policies he advocated but his breaches of decorum, real or alleged. Economically, the revolution signified that a nation of potential money-makers could not abide traditionary, conservative limitations on business enterprise, particularly by capitalists in Philadelphia. The Jacksonian revolution was a consequence of the Industrial Revolution and of a farm-born people's realization that now anyone in America could get rich and through his own efforts, if he had a fair chance. A conception of earned wealth arose which rendered the self-made man as superior morally to the hereditary well-to-do as the agrarian had been. It was like the conception which led Theodoric the Great to boast that he held Italy solely by right of conquest and without the shadow of legal, that is, hereditary right. The humbly born and rugged individualists who were gaining fortunes by their own toil and sweat, or wits, were still simple Americans,

Jeffersonian, anti-monopolistic, anti-governmental, but fraught with the spirit of enterprise and fired with a sense of what soon would be called manifest destiny. They envied the social and economic advantages of the established urban capitalists, mercantile and financial; and they fought these aristocrats with far more zeal and ingenuity than the agrarians ever had. They resented the federal Bank's interference with expansion of the monetary supply. They found it bestriding the path of enterprise, and with Apollyon's brag but Christian's better luck they were resolved to spill its soul. They democratized business under a great show of agrarian idealism and made the age of Jackson a festival of *laisser faire* prelusive to the age of Grant and the robber barons.

In their attack on the Bank of the United States, the Jacksonians still employed the vocabulary of their agrarian backgrounds. The phraseology of idealism was adapted to money-making, the creed of an earlier generation becoming the cant of its successor. Their terms of abuse were "oppression," "tyranny," "monied power," "aristocracy," "wealth," "privilege," "monopoly"; their terms of praise were "the humble," "the poor," "the simple," "the honest and industrious." Though their cause was a sophisticated one of enterpriser against capitalist, of banker against regulation, and of Wall Street against Chestnut, the language was the same as if they were all back on the farm. Neither the President, nor his advisers, nor their followers saw any discrepancy between the concept of freedom in an age of agrarianism and the concept of freedom in one of enterprise. Only the poets and philosophers were really aware that a discrepancy existed and though troubled by it their vision was far from clear. Notwithstanding their language, therefore, the Jacksonians' destruction of the Bank of the United States was in no sense a blow at capitalism or property or the "money power." It was a blow at an older set of capitalists by a newer, more numerous set. It was incident to the democratization of business, the diffusion of enterprise among the mass of people, and the transfer of economic primacy from an old and conservative merchant class to a newer, more aggressive, and more numerous body of business men and speculators of all sorts.

The Jacksonians were unconventional and skillful in politics. In their assault on the Bank they united five important elements, which, incongruities notwithstanding, comprised an effective combination. These were Wall Street's jealousy of Chestnut Street, the business man's dislike of the federal Bank's restraint upon bank credit, the politician's resentment at the Bank's interference with states' rights, popular identification of the Bank with the aristocracy of business, and the direction of agrarian antipathy away from banks in general to the federal Bank in particular. Destruction of the Bank ended federal regulation of bank credit and shifted the money center of the country from Chestnut Street to Wall Street. It left the poor agrarian as poor as he had been before and left the money power possessed of more money and more power than ever.

II

By the term "Jacksonian" I mean not merely the President's Democratic supporters, whom he still called Republican, but in particular his closest advisers and sharers in responsibility. These included most of his "Kitchen Cabinet," some of his official Cabinet, and a number of others. Those most responsible for the destruction of the Bank, without whose urgency and help it might not have been undertaken or achieved, were all either business men or closely concerned with the business world. Named in the approximate order of their appearance, they were Duff Green, Samuel Ingham, Isaac Hill, Martin Van Buren, Amos Kendall, Francis Preston Blair, Churchill C. Cambreleng, Roger B. Taney, and David Henshaw—all but Taney being or becoming men of wealth. They did not include Major William B. Lewis, a Tennessee planter, one of the General's oldest friends and the only one of his intimates not openly hostile to the Bank. Others of importance were Thomas Hart Benton, James K. Polk, Levi Woodbury, Benjamin F. Butler, Jacob Barker, Reuben M. Whitney, William Gouge, and James A. Hamilton*....

III

...With the business interests and objectives of the Jacksonians I have no quarrel save for the cant which made the conflict over the Bank of the United States appear to be one of idealism against lucre and of human rights against property rights. The Jacksonians were no less drawn by lucre than the so-called conservatives, but rather more. They had no greater concern for human rights than the people who had what they were trying to get. The millionaires created by the so-called Jacksonian revolution of "agrarians" against "capitalists"—of the

*In his chapter on the Jacksonians from which this selection is taken, Hammond summarizes the business interests, activities, and philosophy of each of these men, presenting evidence to indicate that all were either business men or closely connected with the business community. See Hammond, *Banks and Politics*, pp. 330-345—Ed.

democracy against the money-power— were richer than those they dispossessed, they were more numerous, they were quite as ruthless; and *laisser faire*, after destroying the monopolies and vested rights the Jacksonians decried, produced far greater ones. There was nothing sacred about the federal Bank. The defense of it is simply that it was very useful and if not perfect it could have been improved, had its enemies felt any interest in improving it. The Jacksonians paid no heed to its merits but canted virtuously about the rich and the poor, hydras, and other irrelevancies. This was good politics. But it cannot conceal the envy and acquisitiveness that were their real motives. What the Jacksonians decided on, they directed their propaganda toward, and got. What they went for, they fetched, like Amos Kendall. An unusual number of them were not only business men but journalists, and gained both profit and influence through the press—notably Duff Green, Amos Kendall, Francis Preston Blair, Isaac Hill, and David Henshaw. They told the world it was governed too much. They vied with their great contemporary James Gordon Bennett [editor of the New York *Herald*] in a glib and vigorous style. The Washington *Globe,* the organ of the administration, was attractively printed on good paper, every active Jacksonian had to take it, and, its contents aside, even the best people could feel satisfied to have it lying on the parlor table.

It relied otherwise on unashamed, repetitious adulation of Andrew Jackson and defamation of his enemies. It presented matters in black and white, Bank and President, hydra and hero. "Many a time," Amos Kendall is made to say in John Pendleton Kennedy's satire, *Quodlibet,* "have I riveted by diligent hammering, a politic and necessary fabrication upon the credulity of the people —so fast that no art of my adversary could tear it away to make room for the truth. Therefore, I say to you and our democratic friends—hammer without ceasing."

IV

... "Andrew Jackson was on the side of the capitalists," writes Mr. Marquis James of his earlier career. "His first case in Nashville in 1788 had landed him as champion of the creditors against the debtors. Jackson desired wealth." He had been opposed to western relief measures taken on behalf of debtors in the ten years preceding his election to the Presidency. They were wicked, pernicious, profligate, and unconstitutional. Opinions like this put him logically on the side of the Bank of the United States, which was the pivotal creditor, and opposed him to the banks made of paper, such as the Bank of the Commonwealth of Kentucky, over which his kitchen adviser, Francis Preston Blair, had presided. But solecisms embarrassed the General very little. On the frontier more than elswhere, the modification of an agrarian economy into an industrial and financial one was such, in William Lyon Mackenzie's words, as to "make speculation as extensive as life, and transform a Jeffersonian democracy into a nation of gamesters and our land into one great gaming house where all are forced to play, while but few can understand the game." General Jackson's prejudices were stronger than his convictions, and he was himself among the least consistent and stable of the Jacksonians. ...

What counts is that Jackson was popular. He was a picturesque folk character, and it does his memory an injustice to make him out a statesman. "All the remodelling and recoloring of Andrew Jackson," says Professor Abernethy, "has not created a character half so fascinating as he was in reality." To the dissatisfied, whether through distress or ambition, Andrew Jackson offered a distinct and attractive change from the old school of leaders the country had had—and not the least by his want of real ideas. He became the champion of the common man, even though the latter might be no longer either frontiersman or farmer but speculator, capitalist, or entrepreneur of a new, democratic sort, who in every village and township was beginning to profit by the Industrial Revolution, the growth of population, and the expanding supply of bank credit. This new common man was manufacturer, banker, builder, carrier, and promoter. He belonged to the "active and enterprising," in the luminous contrast put by Churchill C. Cambreleng, as against the "wealthier classes." And his conflict was not the traditionary one between the static rich and the static poor but a dynamic, revolutionary one between those who were already rich and those who sought to become rich.

General Jackson was an excellent leader in the revolt of enterprise against the regulation of credit by the federal Bank. Though the inferior of his associates in knowledge, he was extraordinarily effective in combat. And as a popular leader he combined the simple agrarian principles of political economy absorbed at his mother's knee with the most up-to-date doctrine of *laisser faire*. Along with several of the best constitutional authorities of his day—but not Mr. Taney—General Jackson believed that the notes issued by state banks were unconstitutional. In 1820 he wrote to his friend Major Lewis: "You know my opinion as to the banks, that is, that the constitution of our state as well as the Constitution of the United States prohibited the establishment of banks in any state. Sir, the tenth section of the first article of the federal Constitution is positive and explicit, and when you read the debates in the convention you will find it was introduced to prevent a state legislature from passing such bills." Seventeen years later, in 1837, he wrote to Senator Benton: "My position now is and has ever been since I have been able to form an opinion on this subject that Congress has no power to charter a Bank and that the states are prohibited from issuing bills of credit or granting a charter by which such bills can be issued by any corporation or order." Yet in effect he did as much as could be done to augment the issue of state bank notes and was proud of what he did. Most statesmen would feel some embarrassment in such a performance.

The Jacksonians were anything but rash. Once decided that they should fight the Bank rather than wed with it, they developed their attack patiently, experimentally, shrewdly, probing the aristocratic victim and teasing public interest into action. The President himself took no unnecessary chances, but those he had to take he took without fear. He was a man of "sagacious temerity," in the words of one of his contemporaries. His attack on the Bank was like his careful slaying of Charles Dickinson in a duel thirty years before. His opponent had been formidable—much younger than he and an expert marksman, which he himself was not. Each was to have one shot. Jackson and his second had gone over the prospects care-

fully and decided it would be best to wait for Dickinson to fire first. For though Jackson would probably be hit, "he counted on the resource of his will to sustain him until he could aim deliberately and shoot to kill, if it were the last act of his life." So he awaited his adversary's fire and, as he had expected, he was hit. But his coat, buttoned loosely over his breast, as was his wont, had presented a deceptive silhouette, and the ball had missed his heart. He concealed his hurt and concentrated on his helpless enemy, whose life he now could take. "He stood glowering at him for an instant, and then his long pistol arm came slowly to a horizontal position." He aimed carefully and pulled the trigger. But the hammer stopped at half-cock. The seconds consulted while the principals stood, and Jackson was allowed to try again. Once more he took deliberate aim, his victim waiting in evident horror, and fired. Dickinson fell, mortally hurt. "I should have hit him," Jackson asserted later, "if he had shot me through the brain." The same mystical will power, the same canny and studious appraisal of probabilities and of relative advantages and disadvantages, weighed in the conflict with the Bank. The President tantalized the frank and impatient Mr. Biddle, he waited for him to make the appropriate mistakes, and then with care and effectiveness he struck. His adversaries' weaknesses were no less at his command than his own skill.

V

Andrew Jackson, a westerner, was not elected by the West alone; New York, where the Republican party had been strong ever since Aaron Burr had contrived to get a bank established that could serve its interests, was an important factor in his election and even more important in his administration. In both houses of Congress the New York delegations included some of his ablest supporters; James A. Hamilton and Martin Van Buren were among his most influential advisers—the former less and less important to him as time went on, the latter more and more. Mr. Van Buren's judgment, skill, and charm gave him remarkable influence over the President personally and over his administration as a whole.

Economically as well as politically New York had gained greatly in importance as compared with Massachusetts, Pennsylvania and Virginia in the forty years of the Republic's existence. New York City had had at first no decisive natural advantages over Philadelphia, long the country's metropolis, except perhaps her more central position on the coastline of the northern states. But the greater commodiousness of her harbor became of decisive importance after the volume of commerce and the tonnage of ships had grown to sufficient magnitudes. By 1820 she surpassed Philadelphia in population. The Erie Canal, completed in 1825, was an audacious and costly exploitation of the state's topographic advantages. It brought New York City an immense and growing western trade and determined her commercial primacy over Philadelphia. Projects of equal importance were impracticable for Pennsylvania, and till railways were constructed Philadelphia's commerce depended on natural conditions. Moreover, Philadelphia, seated between New York and Baltimore, had two rivals for western trade, whereas New York had none but Philadelphia herself. For such reasons opportunity tended to be better for the man of enterprise in New York

than in Philadelphia, and a democratic, dynamic, and competitive expansion of business became characteristic of that city and of the state too. The Albany Regency, perhaps the most efficient party machine in American history, was not parasitical on business, as most political organizations are, but constructive and energizing. Under the quiet, self-effacing, but electric leadership of Martin Van Buren, it devised a symbiosis between business and party in which both prospered.

In 1828 Martin Van Buren, then senator from New York, was elected Governor when Andrew Jackson was elected President. He kept the office only a few weeks and resigning went to Washington to take the office being held for him at the head of Jackson's Cabinet. During his brief Governorship he obtained enactment of a law establishing a Safety Fund system for the insurance of the liabilities of New York banks. This measure, though drawn in very careless form, was of great practical and political importance. It made the banks of the state a system not only strong and worthy of public trust but congenial to the Albany Regency. It gave the people of New York a source of credit which usefully supplemented the Erie Canal as a source of wealth. Both projects were typical of Mr. Van Buren's public policy and both animated it. The Canal, which New York built by herself, rebuked the clamor of poorer and less enterprising states in the West and South for federal aid in such projects. The banking system, centering in Wall Street, cast doubt on the wisdom of maintaining a federal Bank in Philadelphia. Mr. Van Buren's opposition to what he thought misuse of federal powers in both these directions achieved success in two famous vetoes by President

Jackson. The first was the veto in 1830 of a measure authorizing the use of federal funds to build a turnpike between Maysville and Lexington, Kentucky. The second was the veto in 1832 of a measure renewing the charter of the federal Bank. Mr. Van Buren's responsibility for the first was direct and clear; his responsibility for the second was indirect, the forces involved running far beyond his instigation.

Van Buren's policy with respect to federal aid and the federal Bank both reflected his consistent obedience to the constitutional principles of Thomas Jefferson and James Madison. In both, Van Buren opposed Hamiltonian "consolidation" of federal power. He defended states' rights less vocally than John C. Calhoun but not less effectively. Both men had the material interests of their states at heart but both harmonized their championship of those interests with a doctrine that had more than mere expediency to justify it. The federal funds spent on canals and roads elsewhere might diminish New York's particular advantages, which Mr. Van Buren would not brook, but even if they failed to do that they magnified the influence of the federal government, which also, on general grounds, he would not brook.

The Maysville veto was intended to prevent the rise of an abuse; the federal Bank veto was intended to end one already established. The Bank of the United States was not merely another product of unconstitutionally aggrandized federal powers, but, in Van Buren's words, "the great pioneer of constitutional encroachments," the evil growth of federal expansion having begun with Alexander Hamilton's proposals in 1790 for a national Bank. It was the pioneer, but it was also the foremost current exemplar, of federal encroachments. And

besides that it was a material block in the way of New York's interests. Through the state's efforts and those of her leading city, the latter had become a national market for money and commodities and the nerve center of national enterprise. No other community gained from the country's growth as she did or was more prominently identified with its prosperity.

Yet in the federal Bank Philadelphia retained an impressive stronghold of her former primacy. It was the Bank in Philadelphia in whose Wall Street office the revenues of the port of New York were received on deposit. Those revenues, paid by New York businessmen, were larger than those of all other American ports together, but they passed into the control of directors who were mostly Philadelphians. New York's jealousy in this matter was no empty question of first place in an honorific sense but a lively question of whose pockets the profits were going into. It was the Bank in Chestnut Street whose constant regulatory action restrained the freedom of Wall Street's banks to lend what they considered to be their own money and also the freedom of their customers to borrow it. With General Jackson in the White House and the Safety Fund banks under way, a point was reached where something could be done to end the financial subordination of Wall Street to Philadelphia and to the Bank there, whose charter would expire in seven years. Nothing, it would seem, was more deserving Mr. Van Buren's care, on grounds of his personal convictions and the material interests of his state, than that renewal of the federal Bank's charter be prevented....

It is vain of course to look for an open avowal of Mr. Van Buren's purpose. He seldom committed himself and then only in terms as equivocal and disarming as possible. He was a lamb who led lions. Moreover, among the particular and general reasons for ending the Bank of the United States, it was inexpedient to advertise any but the general. An attempt to whip up a country-wide passion for the relief of Wall Street from the tyranny of Chestnut was quite unnecessary and if made would fail. The assault on the Bank must take the conventional form of a popular revolt against privilege—a struggle of the "people" against the "money power"—and a democratic checking of federal encroachments on the constitutional rights of the states. This was managed without too much difficulty and few persons suspected that more was involved than what they heard shouted—especially since capitalists are supposed to stick together, whether in New York or Philadelphia, and to cut the throats of the poor only, not one another's....

The Jacksonians were probably much better agreed about destruction of the existing Bank than about the sequel to it. Some, as will appear, wanted a new Bank as large or larger in New York. Some wanted it in Boston. Andrew Jackson himself apparently would have had it in Washington. Others were interested chiefly in the advantages to be spread among existing banks and new local banks everywhere. In the end the latter view prevailed. No one big new bank was needed in New York to realize the advantages to be gained over Philadelphia, and the preference for local institutions was general.

VI

Despite the fact of a strong and determined rebellion within the business world against the Bank of the United States, the fiction that the attack on the Bank was on behalf of agrarians against capitalists, of humanity against property, of the poor against the rich, and of "the people" against "the money power," has persisted. There was, to be sure, an extremely respectable minority comprising the more conservative and thoughtful men of business, Mr. [Albert] Gallatin, for example, and Nathan Appleton, who defended the Bank till near the end, but it will scarcely do to say that they represented the business world while C. C. Cambreleng, David Henshaw, and Reuben Whitney did not.*

It is obvious that New York, besides gaining most from a successful attack on the Bank, risked the least; for it did not need, as the South and West did, the capital brought in by the Bank's branches. The West's aversion for the federal Bank was like the nationalistic resentment in a 20th century underdeveloped economy which wants and needs imported capital but growls at the "imperialism" of the country that is expected to provide it. The western enemies of the Bank were moved by complex psychological and political considerations—including past distress and present dependence—while its New York enemies were moved, much more simply, by covetousness and rivalry. This was the decisive new ingredient provided in the Jacksonian attack. The agrarian prejudice had been alive since 1791 and most dangerous to the Bank a few years past during its critical days and the distress in the Ohio valley. The state bank opposition was almost as old as

*Appleton was a Massachusetts industrialist and congressman; Henshaw, also of Massachusetts, was a businessman, legislator, and Jacksonian political boss; and Whitney, a New England merchant, was a former director of the Bank of the United States—Ed.

the agrarian. And the relative import-ance of the two varied with the decline of agrarianism and the growth of enter-prise. New York, now the center of enterprise, added to the long-lived an-tagonism a hearty and acute self-interest. That Andrew Jackson proved to be the instrument of her interest was the happy result of Mr. Van Buren's skill and devotion.

It goes without saying that Andrew Jackson himself did not understand what was happening. He had started with a vague, agrarian prejudice against banking which on occasion cropped up throughout his life but never led him to deny himself the service of banks or the friendship and support of bankers.[1] It was no great task for his advisers to arouse this dormant distrust, nourished on what he had read about the South Sea Bubble, and focus it upon the Bank in Philadelphia, a city whence he had suffered years before, at the hands of a bankrupt merchant and speculator, a harsh financial misfortune. Nor was an elaborate plot required to be agreed upon among conspirators. The first harassment of the Bank from the ad-ministration group was evidently spon-taneous and simply aimed at making the Bank Jacksonian. Some time elapsed before it got under directed control. Even then there is no reason to suppose that the program was not mainly op-portunistic. In the early stages the object need have been only to make sure that the charter be not renewed. To this end the General's mind must be fixed

[1] He did not cease transacting personal and family business with the Nashville office of the Bank of the United States, which he presumably dissociated from the main office in Phila-delphia. The view was reasonable. Gravitation of the branches toward independence was a perennial source of weakness to the Bank; and eventually they became local banks in fact.

against the Bank, and the proper im-provement of opportunities could be left to the discretion of those in whose path the opportunities appeared. The adviser who influenced the General most directly or who perhaps left the best record of what he did was Roger B. Taney, though he joined the Jacksonian circle late. He succeeded in filling the General's mind with a vindictiveness that Martin Van Buren or Amos Kendall would probably not have produced. They too would have killed the Bank but with less emotion and less cant. "When a great monied institution," Mr. Taney told the General, "attempts to overawe the President in the discharge of his high constitutional duties, it is conclusive evidence that it is conscious of possessing vast political power which it supposes the President can be made to feel." The Taney reasoning is sound, but the premises are misrepresented, and the effect was to fill the President with bitter suspicion of the Bank; though the alleged "attempts to overawe the Presi-dent"—this was written in June 1832—were the reasonable attempts of Mr. Biddle to gain support for the Bank, find out what the scowls and rumblings from Washington signified, and remove the doubts that he thought were trou-bling the President.

But thanks to the sort of thing Mr. Taney kept telling him, the President by now had few doubts such as Mr. Biddle imagined. He was merely considering how best to proceed against the Bank. Replacement, he realized, was necessary, and for a long time he was fumbling over unintelligible projects to that end. One of these projects, which may be intel-ligible to those whose understanding has not been corrupted by some knowledge and experience of the subject, was des-cribed to James A. Hamilton, 3 June

1830. The President had in mind "a national bank chartered upon the principles of the checks and balances of our federal government, with a branch in each state, the capital apportioned agreeably to representation and to be attached to and be made subject to supervision of the Secretary of the Treasury." He recalls having shown Mr. Hamilton "my ideas on a bank project, both of deposit (which I think the only national bank that the government ought to be connected with) and one of discount and deposit, which from the success of the State Bank of South Carolina I have no doubt could be wielded profitably to our government with less demoralizing effects upon our citizens than the Bank that now exists. But a *national* Bank, entirely *national* Bank of deposit is all we ought to have: but I repeat a national Bank of discount and deposit may be established upon our revenue and national faith pledged and carried on by salaried officers, as our revenue is now collected, with less injury to the morals of our citizens and to the destruction of our liberty than the present hydra of corruption and all the emoluments accrue to the nation as part of the revenue." But these ruminations belonged merely to a period of waiting. As soon as a promising arrangement offered, the President acted. He ordered the federal funds removed from the bank and put in the banks of his friends.

Besides contributing mainly, by this course, to a shift of the money market from Chestnut Street to Wall Street, the General contributed to the inflation, the speculation, and the various monetary evils which, with a persistent agrarian bias, he blamed on banks and paper money. There were plenty of men in his own party, among them better agrarians than himself, who would have

cleared his vision and tried to, but the old gentleman preferred the sycophantic advisers who stimulated his suspicions and prejudices, blinded him to facts, confused him about the nature of the federal Bank's usefulness, diverted his attention from the possibility that it be amended and corrected instead of being destroyed, and allowed him to declaim the most ignorant but popular clap-trap.

VII

Although the Bank was by no means the only thing that occupied the Jacksonians, its destruction was apparently esteemed by many of them their finest accomplishment. It rumpled and demoralized the aristocrats they envied. It redistributed vested rights. It established *laisser faire*. It freed banks from federal credit regulation. It reduced the government's monetary powers by more than half. It stimulated business. It furthered the interests of New York City, Boston, and Baltimore at the expense of Philadelphia. In all this there was abundant satisfaction for Van Buren, Kendall, Henshaw, Cambreleng, Taney, and others who were like-minded....

Popular propaganda has acquired more general and familiar use since the age of Jackson, but none more skillful. With the exception of a few persons who, with John Pendleton Kennedy, could appreciate the art of Amos Kendall and his associates, Americans were hypnotized by the Jacksonian propaganda, and Andrew Jackson himself—its main object—got guidance and inspiration from it. That many historians still follow the Jacksonian formula points to its effectiveness. In the words of one [Ralph Gabriel], for example, "The poor men of the East and of the West were asserting the power of their mass strength and, putting Andrew Jackson in the presidency, were smashing that symbol of financial autocracy, the great Bank of the United States." I take this quotation not as the isolated judgment of one historian but as typical of the view that seems in recent years to have gained in conventional favor, despite the record of the conspicuous business interests of the leading Jacksonians, of the accomplishments of the federal Bank, and of the disposition of the state banking interests toward it, especially in New York and Boston.

The words of another historian [A. M. Schlesinger, Jr.] are equally typical. "By doing away with paper money," he says, Jacksonian policy "proposed to restrict the steady transfer of wealth from the farmer and laborer to the business community. By limiting banks to commercial credit and denying them control over the currency, it proposed to lessen their influence and power. By reducing the proportion of paper money, it proposed to moderate the business cycle, and order the economy to the advantage of the worker rather than the speculator."

These statements seem to me fallacious, individually and collectively. For one thing I do not believe that Van Buren, Kendall, Cambreleng, Henshaw, and Taney ever purposed restricting the transfer of wealth from the farmer and laborer to the business community, or lessening the influence and power of banks, or moderating the business cycle, or ordering the economy to the advantage of the worker. The passage reflects the Jacksonians' views neither of men nor of money. The two latter aims they never thought of, in modern terms, and the two former were nearer the opposite of what they sought. And if Van Buren, Kendall, Cambreleng, Henshaw, and Taney ever supposed that any of these

aims could be achieved by getting rid of paper money and limiting banks to commercial credit, then I shall have to acknowledge that they were less bright than I supposed. They probably understood the equivalence of note and deposit liabilities as well as Albert Gallatin did, and they certainly knew that a greater volume of business payments could be made by check more conveniently than by bank notes, if not already so made. Their attack on banking powers, except as exercised by the federal Bank, was pretense. But it was pretense conveniently obscured by the current confusion as to what comprised banking powers. So long as most people identified banking with note issue, an attack on note issue seemed deadly to bankers and the money power. Instead, it would be bad for bankers in the backwoods, for whom note issue was still important, but the bankers in Wall Street it would never touch.

But, of course, the notion that even the note issue function of banks was seriously threatened was not entertained by any sophisticated Jacksonian. Senator Thomas Hart Benton, it is true, seems to have entertained it, for when in 1837 he saw banks and bank issues increasing, he showed signs of real surprise. "I did not join in putting down the Bank of the United States," he said, "to put up a wilderness of local banks. I did not join in putting down the paper currency of a national bank to put up a national paper currency of a thousand local banks." It is doubtful if many Jacksonian leaders shared his *naïveté*. They may rather have been amused at Old Bullion's primitive ideas.

That the party should have been so largely a party of business enterprise and that its leaders should have been men so devoted to the principle of *laisser faire* is not in itself to be reprehended, of course. Even the critics of that principle can excuse the Jacksonians for being impressed by it. In a sense *laisser faire* was idealistic in that it assumed human nature to be good and governments, save at their simplest, evil. But the preoccupations of *laisser faire* were in fact materialistic. It was the device of men who wished to make money. They clothed their new aspirations in the familiar, idealistic language of the religious and agrarian traditions in which they had been reared. There was no other period in American history, one would hope, when language was more idealistic, endeavor more materialistic, and the tone of public life more hypocritical than during the Jacksonian revolution.

On the Bank itself, of course, the party was divided, though the close associates of the President who befriended it, William B. Lewis, Louis McLane, and Edward Livingston, were exceptional. On the tariff, which rivaled the Bank in importance, the division was far more confusing; though the party was professedly for low tariffs, it was responsible for schedules that provoked the doctrine of nullification. Logically, free trade should have been deduced as directly from Amos Kendall's dictum, "the world is governed too much," as was the quashing of currency and credit regulation, and a substantial number of Jacksonians contended consistently for both, as Cambreleng did. But others, including Jackson himself, and the country as a whole, chose governmental interposition in the form of protective tariffs and rejected it in the form of credit restriction. These were choices that followed the higher logic of what was most profitable: government should boost business but should not bother it—becoming at its

best Hamiltonian in one direction and Jeffersonian in the other. Party-wise, and reduced to the simplest terms, the Jacksonian aims—that is, Mr. Van Buren's—were to end Philadelphia's rivalry of New York as financial center and Mr. Calhoun's rivalry of Mr. Van Buren himself as successor to Andrew Jackson in the presidency. Both aims were achieved, at the sacrifice of monetary regulation on the one hand and of low tariffs on the other.[2]

VIII

Nicholas Biddle, who seems to have been a Jacksonian himself to the extent of having voted for the General in place of his old friend John Quincy Adams, had no such band of helpers to defend the Bank of the United States as General Jackson had to attack it. The older, more conservative, non-political part of the business world supported the Bank with enough decorum but too little energy. Those who defended it the loudest did so because they disliked Andrew Jackson. Henry Clay and Daniel Webster, though they were committed to the Bank on principle, were far more committed to anything that would thwart the General.

Henry Clay was himself a very popular westerner, skillful in politics, ambitious, and able. He too had been a poor boy but singularly fortunate in winning important friends to ease his rise. Except for farming and cattle-breeding, statecraft absorbed him. His policy of fostering American industry with protective tariffs was much approved in the North,

[2] My analysis is the same in substance as Mr. Wiltse's in his biography of Calhoun: "Opposition to internal improvements and opposition to the Bank were the basic economic interests of New York and were therefore the corner stones of Van Buren's policy." Charles M. Wiltse, *John C. Calhoun, Nullifier*, 40; also chap. 10.

though it conflicted in principle and even in practice with *laisser faire.* Clay's policy ultimately prevailed and was of immense consequence to business enterprise, but he was not himself a successful money-maker.

Neither was Daniel Webster. The impracticality and improvidence in business matters of these two brilliant men contrasts interestingly with the shrewd acquisitiveness of their Jacksonian opponents, who knew how to make money and hold on to it. For Henry Clay and Daniel Webster, champions of the "money power," of "monopoly," and of "privilege," were always going beyond their means, floundering in debt, and dependent on their friends to keep them on their feet. Thomas Wren Ward, of Boston, a business man of the foremost ability and character, reported to his principals, the Barings, that he considered Mr. Webster "by far the greatest man we have," and "in bringing power on a given point... probably greater than any man now living." Yet, he also said, "great as Mr. Webster unquestionably is, and sound as are his views generaly, and able as he is on great occasions in defending the true principles of the Constitution and upholding the rights of property, still I do not give him my esteem and confidence." This was because, in Mr. Ward's opinion, he showed "a disregard to his moral obligations and a recklessness in pecuniary matters." Mr. Ward depicts Mr. Webster as living largely by passing the hat among wealthy men, who lent him money because of his public importance and scarcely expected him to repay it; in England he would try to do the same. "It will be easy to have him in your books if you desire it, but whatever he may owe you, I think you will be very safe in writing off to profit and loss."

The two best aides Mr. Biddle had were Horace Binney and John Sergeant, Philadelphia lawyers of great competence. The latter was a personal friend of Nicholas Biddle from the literary days of the *Port Folio.** Neither Binney nor Sergeant had had so golden a social and economic background as Nicholas Biddle, but neither could they be called poor farm boys and self-made men. They were the best of Mr. Biddle's aides in the inadequate sense that they were highly intelligent, judicious, and reputable gentlemen; which, of course, made them no match whatever for President Jackson's array of experts. Unlike Henry Clay and Daniel Webster, they had something of the sincere, understanding loyalty to the Bank that Nicholas Biddle had. They knew its purpose and value as he did. Mr. Webster knew its purpose and value long enough to make a speech; I doubt if Mr. Clay ever bothered to go beyond the simple generalization that the Bank was an important institution which Andrew Jackson did not like.

Politics also kept John C. Calhoun from helping the Bank as he might have done. More than anyone else, he could claim the chartering of the Bank in 1816 as his work, and he understood the Bank's operations better than anyone else in Washington. But just at the time when the assault on the Bank was most critical—in 1832 and 1833—Mr. Calhoun was wholly absorbed in resistance to the tariff. In January 1834, however, he passed a scathing and accurate judgment on removal of the public deposits from the government Bank and on the reasons offered to Congress by Secretary Taney for this removal. In this address and in

*The *Port Folio* was probably the most sophisticated literary periodical in the nation when it published the first contribution of young Nicholas Biddle in 1804 (he was then eighteen). Biddle later became editor of the periodical—Ed.

another in March, no less brilliant, he discussed the functions of the Bank clearly and objectively. His thorough understanding of its functions in the economy was based, as Nicholas Biddle's had originally been, on intelligent study and not at all on experience. Yet even more forcefully than the Bank had ever done he rested his argument where it belonged—on the constitutional responsibility of the government for the currency. He was distinguished among American statesmen in his realization that banking is a monetary function, that regulation of all the circulating medium is the duty of the federal government, and that the duty is to be exercised through a central bank; not for more than a century was such understanding of the subject to be expressed again in Congress. Daniel Webster in particular had never asserted the positive and proper defense of the Bank of the United States as Mr. Calhoun had. His argument was merely legal, not economic.

According to Webster, the Bank was authorized by the Constitution if necessary to the government's operations. This fell far short of seeing in the Bank the one effective means of meeting the federal government's responsibility, under the Constitution, for the circulating medium. Further, Daniel Webster leaned on the jejune defense of vested rights, an obsolescent contention which weakened the Bank's case by the antagonisms it raised and failed entirely to take it off the ground prepared for it by its selfish enemies. Mr. Calhoun's argument, practically alone, put the case on the high, affirmative, responsible ground of monetary powers, where it belonged. But politically it had no effect. The idea that the federal Bank regulated the monetary supply in accordance with the Constitution's assignment of powers made no appeal to people who did not see that bank credit was part of the monetary supply, or, if they did see, were unwilling to have it regulated.

JOHN W. WARD (1922-   ) approaches the problem
of interpreting Andrew Jackson in a somewhat
different manner. Employing the relatively new
interdisciplinary methods embodied in the American
Civilization curriculum, he incorporates the
additional insights provided by the techniques
of such disciplines as literary criticism and social
psychology, thus broadening the dimensions of the
more traditional political and economic interpretations.
Jackson, the hero of the age, symbolized for
Americans all those characteristics that made them
a chosen people, set apart to convert and save
the world. After his victory at New Orleans there
were in reality two Jacksons, one the historical
figure, and the other the symbol in the
American myth.*

Andrew Jackson,
Symbol for an Age

In the preceding sections three concepts—Nature, Providence, and Will—
have been examined separately. These
three ideas with their individual con-
notations do not exhaust the meaning
that Andrew Jackson had for the imagination of his contemporaries, but they
do provide the main structural elements
about which his appeal took shape. They
are, to use a violent metaphor, the idea-
tional skeleton of the ideal Andrew
Jackson.

Two things are to be observed about
the total significance of the concepts,
nature, providence, and will. First, they
possess a dramatic unity; that is, all
three achieve realization through one
figure, Andrew Jackson, who was the

age's hero in a wider sense than has
commonly been recognized. Any student
of American culture will quickly be able
to point to other manifestations at the
time of these three ideas, either singly
or in conjunction with one another. This
is necessarily so and is the best proof of
the point I wish to make: that the
symbolic Andrew Jackson is the creation
of his time. Through the age's leading
figure were projected the age's leading
ideas. Of Andrew Jackson the people
made a mirror for themselves. Now
obviously Andrew Jackson, the man,
offered more tractable material for the
construction of a symbol that carried
the meanings we have discovered in the
ideal Jackson than (say) John Quincy

*From *Andrew Jackson, Symbol for an Age*, by John W. Ward. © 1955 by John
William Ward and reprinted by permission of Oxford University Press, Inc.

Adams could offer. But this is less important than the obvious fact that historical actuality imposed little restriction on the creation of the symbolic role the people demanded Andrew Jackson to play. Without attempting to explore the significance of his remark, Richard Hofstadter has observed that "the making of a democratic leader is not a simple process ... Andrew Jackson ... has often been set down as typical of the democratic frontiersman; but many patent facts about his life fit poorly with the stereotype."[1] This is most obviously the case with the relation of Jackson to nature, as Hofstadter sees. It is no less true, as we have seen, with the ideas of providence and will. But this is only to prove what Carlton J. H. Hayes pointed out some years ago: "Nationalist mythology is not in every detail strictly accurate and literally true—no mythology ever is—but after all its main purpose is didactic, 'for example of life and instruction of manners,' and didacticism need not depend slavishly upon historical or scientific fact. It claims and deserves the wider range of imagination and emotion."[2]

The second point to be made about the ideas, nature, providence, and will, is that in addition to their dramatic unity they possess a logical unity. If only the former were true, if these three ideas had in common only a mode of presentation, one would be quite justified in disentangling them and regarding each by itself as I have done. But the process of examining each idea in isolation is artificial; it is carried out for the purpose of analysis. The concepts,

nature, providence, and will, are organically inter-related; they possess a logical coherence which makes a whole and it is their total configuration that determines the symbol, Andrew Jackson.

As can be seen in most of the quotations already presented in this essay, each concept drew strength from one or both of the other two. In addition each idea usually suggests one or both of the others. For example, the idea of providence is implicit in the tutelary power of nature; the glorification of the will is permissible because providence guarantees that the world is oriented toward good; the anti-traditional aspect of nature nourishes the idea that every man has the making of his own greatness within his own determination. As we saw, the ideas of providence and will co-existed least easily; the idea that the future is your own creation is difficult to reconcile with the idea that the future has been prescribed by God. But it is not surprising that a process of the mind which can dispose of brute fact can likewise ignore the demands of internal logic. It was under the auspices of nature and providence that the cult of the self-made man prospered in America. By making God's favor depend upon each man's exertion, the people of the Age of Jackson easily reconciled personal striving with cosmic determinism, as determinists have done from Puritanism to Communism. It is perhaps possible that an age may have ideals which are mutually destructive but the ideas we have discovered in the image of Andrew Jackson are not. In their integration they make a whole stronger than any constituent part.

It is in their broad tendency, however, that the three concepts, nature, providence, and will, most fully coincide. To whatever degree each idea bolstered the

1 Richard Hofstadter, *The American Political Tradition and the Men Who Made It* (New York, 1949), p. 44.

2 Carlton J. H. Hayes, *Essays on Nationalism* (New York, 1928), p. 110.

others, they were all oriented in a single direction. In an age of widening horizons all three ideas sanctioned a violently activistic social philosophy. In 1815, the year in which Andrew Jackson entered upon a stage already furnished by the American imagination, *Niles' Weekly Register* observed that America was marked by the "almost *universal ambition to get forward.*"[3] The unchecked development of the individual was the chief implication of the ideas of nature, providence, and will. It is in this respect that the figure of Andrew Jackson most completely embodies the spirit of his age.

As representative of the idea of nature, Andrew Jackson acted out the belief that training was unnecessary, that traditional learning was no more than an adornment to native sense. The theoretical result of such an attitude was the depreciation of acquired learning and the appreciation of intuitive wisdom. The practical result was a release of energy. Thought was made subordinate to action. Although it need not have done so, the theme of will tended in the same direction. The belief that man's future was his own creation could logically have led to an emphasis on the training of the individual to assure that he wrought wisely. Actually, however, the glorification of the will minimized the value of learning and training. The reason why Jackson's success was used to prove action more important than thought can be inferred from such articles as one called "Self-Cultivation" (subtitled, "Every Man is the Architect of His Own Fortunes"), in which formal education was maintained to be "but a mere drop in the sea, when compared with that which is obtained in the every-

day journeyings of life."[4] The bias of such a point of view is echoed in the statement that "in the wilds of the West [Jackson] acquired that practical form of thought which led him to look to results, and to what was to be done, rather than to matters of speculation."[5] The argument was the same as the one that made environment subordinate to character: "all the instructions of others can do nothing for a man who does not aid himself and proceed with a fixed purpose."[6] Thus, Jackson was described as "starting in life with a few strong natural endowments, everything besides was, with him, self made. It was he himself that improved what God had bestowed or placed near him."[7] This eulogist had more trouble with the place of providence in the theme of the self-made man than did the person who wrote ecstatically of Jackson's first inauguration that "here, the dignity of man stood forth in bold relief,—man, free and enlightened man—owing nothing to the adventitious circumstances, of birth, or wealth, or extrinsic ornaments—but ennobled by nature—bold in conscious liberty."[8]

The doctrine of nature which relegated the precedents of the past to the ash-heap of history released Americans to act in the present for their glorious future. No people, declared a western editor, "are so ready to make experi-

[3] *Niles' Weekly Register*, IX (December 2, 1815), 238.

[4] Anon., "Self-Cultivation," *The Southern Literary Messenger*, VI (June 1840), 461. Wyllie, "The Cult of the Self-Made Man," *passim*, demonstrates the typical nature of this expression.

[5] *The Daily Union*, July 2, 1845.

[6] John Neal, "Self Reliance and Self Distrust," *Brother Jonathan*, III (October 15, 1842), 202.

[7] Woodbury, "Eulogy," Dusenbery, comp., *Monument*, p. 73.

[8] Anon., "Presidential Inaugurations. Jackson—1829," *The Ladies Magazine and Literary Repository*, V (March 1832), 116.

ments respecting social relations and domestic arrangements, as those of the western country,—none ... are so little fettered by established habits, or ... are less disposed to consider hereditary prejudice and heirlooms which cannot be parted with."[9] For an age eager to claim its future the past was no more than accumulated prejudice and sentimental trinkets. The future of America was in the interior because "foreign influences ... cannot reach the heart of the continent where all that lives and moves is American."[10]

The theme of the will more specifically relegated extrinsic circumstances to a place of minor importance. Joseph G. Baldwin extolled Jackson as "one of the Ironsides. He was built of Cromwell's stuff ... He was incredulous of impossibilities ... He had no thought of failure ... there was no such word as fail. Accordingly [!] there was no such thing as failure in his history."[11] Another asserted there was no failure because Jackson was "a Hercules of action, without learning, except that which was self-taught ... taking [the stakes of life] by main force and commanding success by seizing the prize he sought."[12] A society that

9 *Cincinnati Literary Gazette*, III (June 1825), 193.

10 *McGuffey's Newly Revised Eclectic Fourth Reader* (Cincinnati, 1853), p. 313, cited Mosier, *Making of the American Mind*, p. 34.

11 [Baldwin], ' "Representative Men," ' p. 525. On the same page, Baldwin compares Jackson to Napoleon in describing his will power.

12 Wise, *Seven Decades*, p. 118.

held up for emulation this type as its ideal placed a tremendous burden on the individual. It further increased the individual's personal responsibility by implying, through the theme of nature, that the figuratively new man in America stood at the beginning of time. Both the theme of nature and the theme of will demanded tremendous exertion of the isolated man.

For the weak who might take fright at such a limitless prospect, or for the tender who might recoil from the buccaneering overtones of the theme of self-help, there was always the idea of providence. Man in America could commit himself violently to a course of action because in the final analysis he was not responsible; God was in control. Because it was believed that America had a glorious destiny, a mission, which had been ordained by divine providence, the immensity of the task facing the nation and each citizen was bathed in a glorious optimism.

The massive emotions and psychological sanctions of all three of these ideas, nature, providence, and will, converged in the image of Andrew Jackson. The result was a symbolic figure. The symbol was not the creation of Andrew Jackson from Tennessee, or of the Democratic party. The symbol was the creation of the times. To describe the early nineteenth century as the age of Jackson misstates the matter. The age was not his. He was the age's.

MARVIN MEYERS (1921-   ), like Ward, is determined to discover a more adequate explanation for the Jacksonian appeal. He finds it not in any class or sectional challenge, but in the "expressive role" of politics. A dynamic economy and a liberal society fired the ambition of the American at the same time that rapid and ceaseless change aroused his fears by threatening the stability of his society and the permanence of his accepted values. Jackson appealed to a nation of incipient entrepreneurs by recalling the image of the "Old Republic" with its enduring virtues of integrity, morality, frugality, and simplicity. He spoke "to a society drawn fatally to the main chance" in terms of a return to a lost "agrarian republican innocence."*

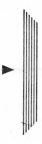

The Restoration of the Old Republic Theme in the Jacksonian Persuasion

On Jackson's Message

On his way toward the presidency Andrew Jackson had gained a splendid military reputation and a loose distinction as the plain man's candidate against the hierarchs of the republican statesmen's club. The broadening of the franchise, the shift to direct choice of presidential electors, the fading of old party lines: all prepared the way for a national hero, combining dramatic flair with the common touch, to break the chain of decorous successions and seize the first place in American political life. The time was ready for the popularity principle to supplant the rule of cabinet promotions in the choice of president; Jackson was precisely the man for the opportunity. His plurality in 1824 and then the decisive majority in 1828 must be regarded first as personal triumphs of the Old Hero, a man whose patriotic deeds, "hickory" character, and exemplary progress from obscurity to fame had wakened a new sort of political enthusiasm. National pride and nascent class ambition were drawn to a natural protagonist.

As Jackson's initial victories were essentially personal, so his early opposition took the form of an ill-matched anti-Jackson junto. Slowly during the first

*Reprinted from *The Jacksonian Persuasion: Politics and Belief* by Marvin Meyers with the permission of the publishers, Stanford University Press. © 1957 by the Board of Trustees of the Leland Stanford Junior University. Footnotes omitted by permission of the author and his publisher.

administration the personal factions, the scattered policy quarrels, entered wider, firmer groupings. With the declaration of the Bank War the Jacksonian Democratic party crystallized: a vastly popular leader and an effective organization had touched the cause which would animate the political life of a generation.

Andrew Jackson did not simply deliver his personal following to the party and shrink into a figurehead. Without his influence the Bank question might have provoked no more than a limited policy argument on familiar grounds. Because he was a commanding figure, and a man of simple, thundering judgments who found things right or wrong and made disputants friends or enemies, the war against the Bank became a general struggle to preserve the values of the Old Republic. A general of the best Roman breed—as partisans saw him —sworn to his people, instinctively just, had come in righteous wrath to strangle a conspiracy with tentacles in every vital part of American society.

One cannot think of Jackson in this situation as the doctrinal counselor, or as the architect of policy. His affirmations and especially his fierce denials have the force of elemental acts: one feels Old Hickory throwing himself into the breach. In his own estimate, and the favorable public's, Jackson was the guardian of a threatened republican tradition which demanded not adjustment or revaluation but right action taken from a solid moral stance. His presidential messages are ragged political philosophy, tendentious accounting, crude policy. Political opponents mocked the contents, but ruefully acknowledged the impressive popular effect. Jackson offered a broad public a moral definition of their situation, a definition that seemed to strike home. Thus Jackson's

messages to Congress and the nation construing out of immediate events the great struggle between people and aristocracy for mastery of the republic, offer a first approach to the appeal of Jacksonian Democracy.

The Real People

Jackson's contemporary rivals damned him for appealing to class against class; some modern writers praise him for it. Beyond question, his public statements address a society divided into classes invidiously distinguished and profoundly antagonistic. But to understand the meaning of this cleavage and this clash, one must see them within a controlling context. There is for Jackson a whole body, the sovereign people, beset with aristocratic sores.

The relentless and apparently irresistible invocation of "the people" in Jacksonian rhetoric is reflected in the diary of a wealthy New York City Whig, Philip Hone, who regularly grinds the phrase through his teeth; or, with accumulated effect, in the growling humor of a Whig delegate to the New York constitutional convention of 1846 "The love of the people, the dear people was all that the gentlemen said influenced them. How very considerate. The love of the people—the dear people—was generally on men's tongues when they wanted to gain some particular end of their own."

In the opposition view Jackson—and Jacksonians generally—were the worst sort of demagogues, men who could appropriate with galling effectiveness both the dignity of the sovereign people and the passion of embattled classes. That is just the point for Jackson. there are the whole people and the alien aristocracy, and the political advantages which result from the use of this distinction further confirm its validity. Jackson's notion of the people as a social class is grounded first in the political order, more precisely in the republican order. From this fixed base, and with this fixed idea of the double character of the people, Jackson's representation of the group composition of society may be analyzed first as an expression of political democracy; and then—by what seems to me a necessary extension—as a judgment of the values which attach to distinct social situations.

In the most inclusive and high-toned usage, the peole would comprise "all classes of the community" and "all portions of the Union." From their midst arises a general "will of the American people," which is something considerably more than a fluctuating majority vote (though the vote for Jackson is acknowledged as a fair index). There are interests of a class and sectional character, legitimate and often illegitimate; but also a pervasive common interest (which corresponds neatly with the main items of the Democratic platform). The general will is originally pure ("Never for a moment believe that the great body of the citizens of any State or States can deliberately intend to do wrong"); liable to temporary error through weakness (corruptionists will sometimes succeed in "sinister appeals to selfish feelings" and to "personal ambition"); and, in the end, straight and true ("but in a community so enlightened and patriotic as the people of the United States argument will soon make them sensible of their errors").

A brief, sharp application of this view occurs in Jackson's argument for direct election of the president. The extent of American territory—Madison's chief reliance for controlling the threat of ma-

jority faction—suggests to Jackson the dangerous prospect of sectional parties, which in turn will present sectional candidates and, in the zeal for party and selfish objects, "generate influences unmindful of the general good." Evil comes from the official apparatus, the mechanical contrivances of the complex electoral system. However, "the great body of the people," armed with a direct presidential vote which can express the general "will," must always defeat "antirepublican" tendencies and secure the common good.

These "antirepublican" forces are identified as the "intriguers and politicians" and their tools, who thrive on political consolidation, chartered privilege, and speculative gain. Jackson sums up their purposes in relation to the Bank War:

The bank is, in fact, but one of the fruits of a system at war with the genius of all our institutions—a system founded upon a political creed the fundamental principle of which is a distrust of the popular will as a safe regulator of political power, and whose ultimate object and inevitable result, should it prevail, is the consolidation of all power in our system in one central government. Lavish public disbursements and corporations with exclusive privileges would be its substitutes for the original and as yet sound checks and balances of the Constitution—the means by whose silent and secret operation a control would be exercised by the few over the political conduct of the many by first acquiring that control over the labor and earnings of the great body of the people. Wherever this spirit has effected an alliance with political power, tyranny and despotism have been the fruit.

From these rough outlines one can derive the gross political conception of the people and the classes which Jacksonians carried into party battle. But Jackson's categories do not remain abstract units in a formal democratic scheme. In political terms the people are the great social residuum after alien elements have been removed. To gain a sense of their nurture and character, as portrayed in Jackson's messages, is to learn the qualities Jacksonians honored. The theme of people vs. aristocracy, when concrete references were added, began to speak of broad opposing social values.

When Jackson writes of the people—"the real people"—he specifies planters and farmers, mechanics and laborers, "the bone and sinew of the country." Thus a composite class of industrious folk is marked off within society. It appears to be a narrower group than "the sovereign people" of democratic doctrine, though it would surely encompass the mass of inhabitants of the Jacksonian era. Historians who identify the favored Jacksonian class simply as the common man tell too little. Others, who make the separation between wage earners and capitalists, or by rich/poor, town/country, East/West, or North/South, accept what seem to me variable secondary traits. Jackson's "real people" are essentially the four specific occupational groups he names, the men whose "success depends upon their own industry and economy," who know "that they must not expect to become suddenly rich by the fruits of their toil." The lines are fixed by the moral aspects of occupation.

Morals, habit, character, are key terms in Jackson's discussion of the people—and almost every other subject. Major policies, for instance, are warranted by their capacity to "preserve the morals of the people," or "to revive and perpetuate those habits of economy and simplicity which are so congenial to the character of republicans." And so with the differentiation of classes according to worth: the American "laboring classes" are "so proudly distinguished" from their for-

eign counterparts by their "independent spirit, their love of liberty, their intelligence, and their high tone of moral character." At a still higher level within the bloc of favored classes, those who work the land—"the first and most important occupation of man"—contribute to society "that enduring wealth which is composed of flocks and herds and cultivated farms" and themselves constitute "a hardy race of free citizens."

The positive definition of the "real people" significantly ignores pursuits which are primarily promotional, financial, or commercial. This does not mean that Jackson raises a class war against mere or whole occupational categories. (He was himself lawyer, officeholder, land speculator, and merchant at various times.) The point seems to be that virtue naturally attaches to, and in fact takes much of its definition from, callings which involve some immediate, responsible function in the production of goods. Vice enters most readily through the excluded pursuits, though it may infect all classes and "withdraw their attention from the sober pursuits of honest industry." Defective morals, habits, and character are nurtured in the trades which seek wealth without labor, employing the stratagems of speculative maneuver, privilege-grabbing, and monetary manipulation.

Like the Jeffersonians, Jackson regularly identifies the class enemy as the money power, the moneyed aristocracy, and so forth. There is in these words undoubtedly some direct appeal against the rich, yet I would maintain that this is a secondary meaning. First, Jackson's bone-and-sinew occupational classes clearly allow for a considerable income range: it would be fair to say that upper-upper and lower-lower would enter only as exceptions, while there would be a heavy concentration at some middling point of independence. Income as an index of differential economic or power interest does not become a ground for the judgment of classes. Instead, Jackson links income with good and evil ways. The "real people" cannot expect sudden riches from their honest, useful work; and surplus wealth would in any case prove a temptation to antirepublican habits of idleness and extravagance. Briefly, a stable income of middling proportions is generally associated with the occupations, and with the habits, morals, and character, of the "real people."

More important, however, is the meaning given to phrases like "money power" —and note that Jackson typically uses this expression and not "the rich." The term occurs invariably in discussions of corporations, particularly banking corporations; it signifies the *paper* money power, the *corporate* money power—i.e., concentrations of wealth arising suddenly from financial manipulation and special privilege; ill-gotten gains. If the suggestion persists in Jackson's public statements that such is the common way to large wealth, and certainly the only quick way, then it is still the mode and tempo of acquisition, and not the fact of possession, which is made to damn the rich before Jackson's public.

Further, the money power is damned precisely as a *power*, a user of ill-gotten gains to corrupt and dominate the plain republican order. Any concentration of wealth may be a potential source of evil; but the real danger arises when the concentration falls into hands which require grants of special privilege for economic success. A wealthy planter (and Jackson was this, too) should need no editorial or legislative hired hands;

a wealthy banker of this era cannot do without them, where incorporation requires special charter grants.

Thus, Jackson's representation of the "real people" in the plain republican order supplies at least tentative ground for an interpretation of Jacksonian Democracy as, in vital respects, an appeal to an idealized ancestral way. Beneath the gross polemical image of people vs. aristocracy one finds the steady note of praise for simplicity and stability, self-reliance and independence, economy and useful toil, honesty and plain dealing. These ways are in themselves good, and take on the highest value when they breed a hardy race of free citizens, the plain republicans of America.

The familiar identification of Jacksonian Democracy and its favored folk with the West has its points, but not when it blends into the image of the raw West. Jackson shows little sympathy for the rural operator, or the rootless mover and claim-jumper. Nor does the moral restoration projected in his public papers bear any resemblance to American primitivism in the Davy Crockett mode. Neither the forest shadows, nor the half-man, half-alligator tone, nor a wild-woods democracy lies at the heart of the Jacksonian persuasion. Rather, one sees a countryside of flocks and herds and cultivated farms, worked in seasonal rhythm and linked in republican community.

Hard Coin and the Web of Credit

As a national political phenomenon, Jacksonian Democracy drew heavily upon the Bank War for its strength and its distinctive character. The basic position Andrew Jackson established for the Democratic party in relation to money and banking continued to operate as a source of political strength through the 1840's. So powerful, in fact, was the Jacksonian appeal that large sections of the rival Whig party finally capitulated on this issue explicitly for the purpose of saving the party's life. First shrewd Whig party managers like Weed of New York, and later most Whig spokesmen, were forced to sacrifice their policy convictions to escape identification as the "Bank Party."

Jackson's standard case against banking and currency abuses has already been sketched above. Within the matrix of his Bank War, the crucial class split is discovered and the general principles of Jacksonian Democracy take shape. However, the Bank War, viewed as a struggle for possession of men's minds and loyalties, does not simply offer a self-evident display of its own meaning. Out of the polemical language there emerges a basic moral posture much like the one which enters Jackson's representation of the republican order.

Jackson's appeal for economic reform suggests at bottom a dismantling operation: an effort to pull down the menacing constructions of federal and corporate power, and restore the wholesome rule of "public opinion and the interests of trade." This has the sound of laissez faire, but with peculiar overtones which give the argument a new effect. Poor Richard and the man on the make may share a common enemy with Jackson's plain republican; indeed the forest democrat, the poor man, and the workingman —social types variously proposed as natural supporters of Jacksonian Democracy—might see their several adversaries overthrown in Jackson's rhetoric. Yet, if Jackson gives promise of catching every man's particular enemy in a broad

aristocracy trap, does he not promise still more powerfully a reformation and a restoration: a return to pure and simple ways?

Tocqueville, though he reaches an opposite conclusion, suggests very effectively this dismantling spirit:

The bank is a great establishment, which has an independent existence; and the people, accustomed to make and unmake whatsoever they please, are startled to meet with this obstacle to their authority. In the midst of the perpetual fluctuation of society, the community is irritated by so permanent an institution and is led to attack it, in order to see whether it can be shaken, like everything else.

But what is it about the great establishment which provokes hostility and a passion for dismantling? How can the permanence of the Bank, set over against the perpetual fluctuation of society, explain the ceaseless Jacksonian complaint against the tendency of the bank precisely to introduce perpetual fluctuation in the economic affairs of society? There is, I think, another and better explanation of the symbolic import of the Bank War.

The Bank of the United States, veritable incarnation of evil in Jackson's argument, assumes the shape of "the Monster," the unnatural creature of lust for wealth and power. Its managers, supporters, and beneficiaries form the first rank of the aristocracy: the artificial product of legislative prestidigitation. The Monster thrives in a medium of paper money, the mere specter of palpable value. The bank system suspends the real world of solid goods, honestly exchanged, upon a mysterious, swaying web of speculative credit. The natural distributive mechanism, which proportions rewards to "industry, economy, and virtue," is fixed to pay off the insider and the gambler.

To knock down this institution, then, and with it a false, rotten, insubstantial world, becomes the compelling object. Jackson removed the public deposits, so he said, "to preserve the morals of the people, the freedom of the press, and the purity of the elective franchise." Final victory over the Bank and its paper spawn "will form an era in the history of our country which will be dwelt upon with delight by every true friend of its liberty and independence," not least because the dismantling operation will "do more to revive and perpetuate those habits of economy and simplicity which are so congenial to the character of republicans than all the legislation which has yet been attempted."

The Jacksonian appeal for a dismantling operation and the restoration of Old Republican ways flows easily into the hard coin argument. Hard coin, I have already suggested, stands for palpable value as against the spectral issue of the printing press. In plainer terms, Jackson argues before the Congress: "The great desideratum in modern times is an efficient check upon the power of banks, preventing that excessive issue of paper whence arise those fluctuations in the standard of value which render uncertain the rewards of labor." Addressing a later Congress, Jackson pursues the point: Bank paper lacks the stability provided by hard coin; thus circulation varies with the tide of bank issue; thus the value of property and the whole price level are at the mercy of these banking institutions; thus the laboring classes especially, and the "real people" generally, are victimized, while the few conniving speculators add to their riches.

A related appeal to the attractions of stability, of sure rewards and steady values and hard coins, can be found in Jackson's belated warnings against the accumulation and distribution of the revenue surplus: an overflowing federal treasury, spilling into the states, would produce ruinous expansions and contractions of credit, arbitrary fluctuations in the price of property, "rash speculation, idleness, extravagance, and a deterioration of morals." But above all it is the banks and their paper system which "engender a spirit of speculation injurious to the habits and character of the people," which inspire "this eager desire to amass wealth without labor," which turn even good men from "the sober pursuits of honest industry." To restore hard coin is to restore the ways of the plain republican order. Dismantling of the unnatural and unjust bank and paper system is the necessary first step.

The Sum of Good Government

The one indispensable credential of public or private worth, whether of individual, or class, or trade, is conveyed by Jackson by the term "republican"; that which is antirepublican is the heart of evil. With all valuations referred to the republican standard, and that standard apparently a category of politics, one might expect some final revelation of the Jacksonian persuasion in Jackson's representation of the good state. The truth is, on my reading, somewhat different. The good republic he portrays—and remembers from the Revolutionary days of 1776 and 1800—is on the political side the ornament, the glory, and the final security of the worthy community, not its creator.

Jackson's sketch of a political system congenial to Old Republican ways uses nothing beyond the memorable summation in Jefferson's First Inaugural Address: "a wise and frugal government, which shall restrain men from injuring one another, shall leave them otherwise free to regulate their own pursuits of industry and improvement, and shall not take from the mouth of labor the bread it has earned. This is the sum of good government, and this is necessary to close the circle of our felicities." The literal Jacksonian translation prescribes: the Constitution strictly construed; strict observance of the "fundamental and sacred" rules of simplicity and economy; separation of political authority from the conduct of economic affairs.

Jackson's political remarks both parallel and support the general themes discussed in previous sections. His ideal is no government of projects and ambitions. It does its simple, largely negative business in a simple, self-denying way. Republican government must be strong, and yet avoid the elaboration of state machinery which would create an autonomous center of power. The hardy race of independent republicans, engaged in plain and useful toil, need no more than a stable government of equal laws to secure their equal rights. In Jacksonian discourse, government becomes a fighting issue only when it grows too fat and meddlesome. Again, the republic is defined and judged positively by its republicans and only negatively by its government.

The Bank War once more provides the crucial case. Jackson mobilized the powers of government for what was essentially a dismantling operation. His cure rejects any transference of the powers of the Bank to another central agency: to give the president the currency controls and the power over individuals now held by the bank "would be as objectionable and as dangerous as to leave it as it is." Control of banks and currency, apart from the strictly constitutional functions of coinage and regulation of value, should be "entirely separated from the political power of the country." Any device is wicked and dangerous which would "concentrate the whole moneyed power of the Republic in any form whatsoever." We must, above all, ignore petty, expedient considerations, and "look to the honor and preservation of the republican system."

A Summary Appraisal

In reopening the most obvious political source I have not intended to rehearse established facts about Jackson's policies and principles. Quite simply, I have examined the presidential messages again within a special framework: assessed them as a political appeal which brought passing events under judgment, in the language of prevalent attitudes and beliefs.

At the level of explicit doctrine, Jackson's message seems to attack manifest violations of formal republican rules. Immediately, however, his rhetoric creates the great, essential opposition of the people and the aristocracy. The people, as a formal political category, becomes the "real people," with characteristic social virtues: the defining traits of the ideal yeoman-republican. The aristocracy, first specified as a definite privilege-holding clique, grows into a diffuse class with pervasive social vices: the mixed attributes of aristocratic arrogance, financial jobbery, and irresponsibly adventurous enterprise.

When the inexorable Old General pits himself against the Bank, he gives political urgency to the encounter of broad social principles. Through his messages and actions the Bank becomes the enemy at the gate, threatening destruction to the city of republican virtue: the commonwealth of plain, honest freemen; of simple, stable, visible economic relationships; of limited and frugal democratic government. Political supporters of the Bank merge with the class which lives on privilege, deceit, and speculation. The party of the president absorbs "the bone and sinew of the country": the farmers and mechanics conditioned by their concrete situation to sustain the values of the Old Republic. Thus Jackson gives to the party contest the aura of a class struggle, distinguishing the classes not by their economic position as such, but primarily by their moral orientation.

One can deflate this rhetoric of moral crisis and incipient social war by insisting that the heart of Jackson's message was in its literal doctrinal formulas and in its limited action-clauses. Briefly: Jackson employed a conventional liberal argument against legal privilege and public economic meddling and latitudinarian construction of constitutional powers; he directed public policy against the Bank monopoly, against federal participation in local improvement projects, against excessive tariffs, public debt, and the use of public lands to furnish revenues for public spending. So Jackson reasoned, so he chose to act: the fact remains that his appeal swept over such confinements.

Andrew Jackson took his liberal political dicta from the previous generation, and with them took an image of the good republican life. Laissez-faire notions were embedded in a half-remembered, half-imagined way of life. When government governed least, society—made of the right republican materials—would realize its own natural moral discipline.

In America, Jacksonians announced, the people were the true conservatives. The liberalism of Jackson's message did not communicate a liberating purpose: there was no vision of a fresh creation at the Western edge of civilization, certainly no dream of enterprise unbound. The rule of equal liberty served to condemn the aristocracy of privilege for sapping republican political institutions, and so to fix an enemy who could bear responsibility for the general erosion of republican social values.

In an age of violent growth and change, Jackson's appeal felt for the uncertainties and suspicions, the actual grievances, perhaps the latent guilts, of his people. He provided a dramatic definition of their discontents. The world of independent producers, secure in their modest competence, proud in their natural dignity, confirmed in their yeoman character, responsible masters of their fate—the order of the Old Republic—was betrayed. From the great visible centers of private wealth and power, a web of economic and political influence reached into every community, threatened every household in the land. Banks and corporations, with their paper mysteries, their secret hold on public men, their mask of anonymity, their legal untouchability, held invisible powers over the life of the community, greater even than their manifest controls.

Between its minimum and maximum terms the Jacksonian appeal could promise much for little: it would destroy the Monster Bank, and it would restore a precious social enterprise to its original purity. With one courageous local amputation, society could save its character—and safely seek the goods it hungered for.

For the Reader Who
Wishes to Probe Further

An indispensable introduction to the subject is Charles G. Sellers, "Andrew Jackson versus the Historians," *Mississippi Valley Historical Review*, XLIV (March 1958), 615-634. A helpful guide in the selection and organization of the extensive literature is the bibliographical essay in Glyndon Van Deusen, *The Jacksonian Era, 1828-1848* (New York, 1959), 267-283.

The various works from which the selections in this volume have been taken should be read in full. The reader who consults the published sources will not only familiarize himself with the writings of Jackson and his contemporaries, but will obtain a better perspective from which to judge the varied interpretations. The correspondence, diaries, and memoirs of several of the leading participants will be found listed in Van Deusen, page 269. New editions of the works of John Q. Adams, Calhoun, Clay, and Madison are now being published and will eventually supplant the older collections of these men cited by Van Deusen. Two convenient and worthwhile source collections not cited are Joseph L. Blau (ed.), *Social Theories of Jacksonian Democracy* (New York, 1954), and Harold C. Syrett (ed.), *Andrew Jackson: His Contributions to the American Tradition* (Indianapolis, 1953). Both contain helpful introductions.

Lest the reader mistakenly assume, from the organization of this volume, that the five interpretive schools cited here constitute the entire literature of the subject, or that all writers within a particular school agree completely with one another, he should consult additional representatives of each school. William G. Sumner, *Andrew Jackson As A Public Man: What He Was, What Chances He Had, and What He Did With Them* (Boston, 1882), spoke for the patrician school as did Parton, included in this pamphlet, and Herman E. Von Holst, *The Constitutional and Political History of the United States*, 8 vols. (Chicago, 1876-1892). Yet each differed in his appraisal of Old Hickory and his followers. M. Ostrogorski's two volumes entitled *Democracy and the Organization of Political Parties* (New York, 1902) should be added to the list. Yet, in several respects, he differs from each of the others.

No student of Jackson can ignore Frederick J. Turner. His interpretation, embodied in *The Frontier in American History* (New York, 1920, 1962), and *The United States, 1830-1850: The Nation and Its Sections* (New York, 1935), influenced all later writers of the Democratic agrarian school. Even such transitional figures as Woodrow Wilson, *A History of the American People*, 5 vols. (New York, 1902), and William MacDonald, *Jacksonian Democracy, 1829-1837* (New York, 1906), whose interpretations were in part influenced by the patrician school, acknowledged their debt to Turner by emphasizing the influence of the West in the democratic upheaval they believed an integral part of the movement. Both Vernon Parrington, included in this pamphlet, and Charles and Mary Beard, *The Rise of American Civilization*, 2 vols. (New York, 1927), owed a similar debt, although their accounts noted the significance of classes as well as sections in the movement. And thanks, at least in part, to Turner, Carl R. Fish, *The Civil Service and the Patronage* (Cambridge, Mass., 1904), would interpret the removal policies of the Jacksonians in a completely different manner than did Parton and Von Holst. Later biographers reflect the same influence. Bassett emphasized Jackson's "masterly leadership of the democratic movement," and Marquis James, *The Life of Andrew Jackson*, 2 vols. (Indianapolis, 1933, 1937), painted a warm and highly sympathetic portrait of Old Hickory as soldier, patriot, and democrat. The height of pro-Jackson partisanship was reached with the publication of Claude G.

Bowers, *The Party Battles of the Jackson Period* (Boston, 1922). The adoption of the democratic frame of reference also caused such political scientists as Leonard White and Wilfred E. Binkley, *American Political Parties: Their Natural History* (New York, 1943), to wield a sympathetic pen in behalf of the Jacksonians.

The writings of the new critical school of Jackson scholars range in time from the publication of Thomas P. Abernethy's article, "Andrew Jackson and the Rise of South-western Democracy," *American Historical Review*, XXXIII (October 1927), 64-77, to the present. They vary in interpretation from the mildly critical approach of Glyndon G Van Deusen, *The Jacksonian Era, 1828-1848* (New York, 1959), to the bitterly hostile attacks of Richard R. Stenberg, whose articles may be found listed in Sellers, page 623, note 18. The judicious and scholarly restraint evident in such biographies as Glyndon G. Van Deusen, *The Life of Henry Clay* (Boston, 1937); Oliver P. Chitwood, *John Tyler* (New York, 1939); and Samuel F. Bemis, *John Quincy Adams and the Union* (New York, 1956), lends to these works an aura of considerable impartiality. This is less evident in the more critical approach of Albert Beveridge, *John Marshall*, 4 vols. (Boston, 1916-1919); Claude M. Fuess, *Daniel Webster*, 2 vols. (Boston, 1930); Reginald C. McGrane, *The Panic of 1837* (Chicago, 1924); Holmes Alexander, *The American Talleyrand: The Career and Contemporaries of Martin Van Buren, Eighth President* (New York, 1935); and Thomas P. Govan, *Nicholas Biddle: Nationalist and Public Banker, 1786-1844* (Chicago, 1959).

By no means all of the scholars, early or recent, belong to the new critical school. Indeed, a rather large group of biographers should be placed in a separate group which displays a partiality to the Jacksonians. Included in such a group would be Edward M. Shepard, *Martin Van Buren* (Boston, 1889); William E. Smith, *The Francis Preston Blair Family in Politics*, 2 vols. (New York, 1933); Carl B Swisher, *Roger B. Taney* (New York, 1936); William B. Hatcher, *Edward Livingston: Jeffersonian Republican and Jacksonian Democrat* (Baton Rouge, 1940); John A. Garraty, *Silas Wright* (New York, 1949); William N. Chambers, *Old Bullion Benton, Senator From the New West* (Boston, 1956);

and Charles G. Sellers, Jr., *James K. Polk, Jacksonian, 1795-1843* (Princeton, 1957).

Strongly pro-Jackson is the book by Arthur Schlesinger, Jr., whose interpretation of the role played by labor and its spokesmen stirred up an ardent debate from which emerged the entrepreneurial school. In addition to Bray Hammond, it includes Richard B. Morris, Edward Pessen, and William A. Sullivan, whose articles are listed in Sellers, pages 627-628, notes 27 and 28, Richard Hofstadter, whose essay on Jackson in his *American Political Tradition and the Men Who Made It* (New York, 1948) contains an excellent brief summary of the entrepreneurial interpretation; and especially Joseph Dorfman, *The Economic Mind in American Civilization*, 3 vols. (New York, 1946-1949) and "The Jackson Wage-Earner Thesis," *American Historical Review*, LIV (January 1949), 296-306.

Additional information relevant to these two opposing views may be obtained by consulting Oscar and Mary F. Handlin, *Commonwealth: A Study of the Role of Government in the American Economy: Massachusetts, 1774-1861* (Cambridge, Mass., 1947); Louis Hartz, *Economic Policy and Democratic Thought: Pennsylvania, 1776-1860* (Cambridge, Mass., 1948); Milton S. Heath, *Constructive Liberalism: The Role of the State in Economic Development in Georgia to 1860* (Cambridge, Mass., 1954); and James N. Primm, *Economic Policy in the Development of a Western State: Missouri, 1820-1860* (Cambridge, Mass., 1954).

Other significant state studies include A. B. Darling, *Political Changes in Massachusetts, 1824-1828* (New Haven, 1925); J. M. Morse, *A Neglected Period of Connecticut's History, 1818-1850* (New Haven, 1933); W. R. Fee, *The Transition From Aristocracy to Democracy in New Jersey, 1789-1829* (Somerville, Mass., 1933); Dixon R. Fox, *The Decline of the Aristocracy in the Politics of New York* (New York, 1919), Robert V. Remini, *Martin Van Buren and the Making of the Democratic Party* (New York, 1959); Walter Hugins, *Jacksonian Democracy and the Working Class: A Study of the New York Workingmen's Movement, 1829-1837* (Stanford, 1960); Lee Benson, *The Concept of Jacksonian Democracy: New York as a Test Case* (Princeton, 1961); Philip Klein, *Pennsylvania Politics, 1817-1832; a Game Without*

Rules (Philadelphia, 1940); Charles M. Snyder, *The Jacksonian Heritage: Pennsylvania Politics, 1833-1848* (Harrisburg, 1958);

Henry H. Simms, *Rise of the Whigs in Virginia, 1824-1840* (Richmond, 1929); William S. Hoffmann, *Andrew Jackson and North Carolina Politics* (Chapel Hill, 1958); Paul Murray, *The Whig Party in Georgia, 1825-1853* (Chapel Hill, 1948); Fletcher M. Green, *Constitutional Development in the South Atlantic States, 1776-1860* (Chapel Hill, 1930); Charles S. Sydnor, *The Development of Southern Sectionalism, 1819-1848* (Baton Rouge, 1948).

Some knowledge of related developments will give the reader a deeper understanding of the Jacksonian movement. Chilton Williamson traces the broadening of the suffrage in *American Suffrage: From Property to Democracy, 1760-1860* (Princeton, 1960). Grant Foreman tells the tragic story of the result of Jackson's Indian policy in *Indian Removal: The Emigration of the Five Civilized Tribes* (Norman, Okla., 1932). E. Malcolm Carroll discusses the formation of an opposition in *Origins of the Whig Party* (Durham, 1925); while Alice F. Tyler summarizes the reform movements of the era in *Freedom's Ferment: Phases of American Social History to 1860* (Minneapolis, 1944). Marcus L. Hansen, *The Atlantic Migration, 1607-1860* (Cambridge, Mass., 1940), deals with the important aspect of immigration. The economic aspects of the period are summarized admirably in George R. Taylor, *The Transportation Revolution, 1815-1860* (New York, 1951). V. S. Clark, *History of Manufactures in the United States, 1607-1928*, 3 vols. (New York, 1929) is a comprehensive but encyclopedic survey; John R. Commons and others, *History of Labour in the United States*, 4 vols. (New York, 1918) is essential for labor in this period; while Selig Perlman, *A History of Trade Unionism in the United States* (New York, 1922), and Foster R. Dulles, *Labor in America: A History* (New York, 1949), while less comprehensive than Commons, are more convenient summaries.

Finally, any person interested in this subject is urged to read carefully the two volumes by Alexis de Tocqueville, *Democracy in America,* now available in a convenient paperback edition (New York: Vintage, 1954). This perceptive Frenchman gives the reader a penetrating insight into Jacksonian America that is almost unique. Nor should any student fail to read the provocative chapter, "The Whig Dilemma," in a fascinating book by Louis Hartz, *The Liberal Tradition in America: An Interpretation of American Political Thought Since the Revolution* (New York, 1955), 89-113. A provocative interpretive essay on the historical literature by John Ward, entitled "The Age of the Common Man," may be found in John Higham, ed., *The Reconstruction of American History* (New York, 1962), 82-97.